WALES

EXPLORING WOODLAND

WALES

Edited by Steven Kind & Graham Blight

F

FRANCES LINCOLN LIMITED
PUBLISHERS

Acknowledgements

Introduction by Archie Miles
Site entries written by Sheila Ashton
Researched by Steven Kind and Lorraine Weeks
Edited by Steven Kind & Graham Blight
Maps by Linda M Dawes, Belvoir Cartographics & Design
Regional maps created using Maps in Minutes data © MAPS IN MINUTES™ 2004.
© Crown Copyright, Ordnance Survey 2004
Site maps © Frances Lincoln Ltd

Photographic acknowledgements

All photographs by Steven Kind except those listed below
Stuart Handley/Foto45: 96
Woodland Trust: 60, 68 (M Taylor), 69 (Pete Holmes), 79 (Mike Brown), 101 (Keith Huggett), 104 (Kenneth Watkins)

Frances Lincoln Ltd
4 Torriano Mews
Torriano Avenue
London NW5 2RZ
www.franceslincoln.com

Wales
Copyright © Frances Lincoln 2006
Text © Woodland Trust 2006
Maps © see above

First Frances Lincoln edition: 2006

A catalogue record for this book is available
from the British Library.

ISBN 10: 0-7112-2662-8
ISBN 13: 978-0-7112-2662-3

Printed and bound in Singapore
The paper used in this book was sourced from
sustainable forests, managed according to FSC
(Forest Stewardship Council) guidelines.

1 2 3 4 5 6 7 8 9

Half title page Aber Falls
Title page Coed Cymerau

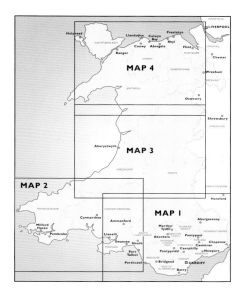

Contents

How to use this guide

Covering the whole of Wales, this book is divided into four areas represented by key maps on pages 18–19, 44–45, 76–77 and 106–107. The tree symbols on these maps denote the location of each wood. In the pages following the key maps, the sites nearest one another are described together (wherever practical) to make planning a day out as rewarding as possible.

For each site entry the name of the nearest town/village is given, followed by road directions and the grid reference of the site entrance. The area of the site (in hectares followed by acres) is given together with the official status of the site where appropriate and the owner, body or organisation responsible for maintaining the site. Symbols are used to denote information about the site and its facilities as explained in the next column.

Type of wood

Mainly broadleaved woodland
Mainly coniferous woodland
Mixed woodland

Car park

Parking on site
Parking nearby
Parking difficult to find

Official status

Area of Outstanding Natural Beauty
AONB
Site of Special Scientific Interest SSSI

Site facilities

Sign at entry
Information board
One or more paths suitable for
  wheelchair users
Dogs allowed under supervision
Waymarked trail
Toilet
Picnic area
Entrance/car park charge
Refreshments on site

Exploring Woodland in Wales

Cwmcarn Forest

From my home in Herefordshire I can look west and see the long straight back of the Black Mountains with its distinctive step down to the book town of Hay-on-Wye. The omnipresence of this natural border with Wales always makes me feel in touch with that other land. In much the same way that a trip down the Wye valley, picking up the river at Monmouth, and exploring the broad meanders of its final few miles to the sea near Chepstow, makes me feel like I've straddled two lands, two cultures, but somehow one magnificent yet complex landscape entirely.

As the road weaves from the lee of the Forest of Dean, over the graceful iron span of Bigsweir bridge on to the Welsh side of the valley, the woodland experience is equally stunning wherever your river flows. The Lower Wye Valley woods constitute one of the finest ravine woodland systems in the whole of Europe. These semi-natural ancient woods contain all manner of splendid trees, including massive old lime, beech and ash, along with yew trees growing from improbable rocky clefts and a few rare hornbeams peculiar to one or two very localised sites in the southern reaches of the borders. Nationally important species such as lesser horseshoe bats, dormice and the elusive white admiral butterfly can be found here and, as its name might suggest, the local Tintern spurge is a special plant to seek out. The Wye Valley Walk will actually take you right to the source near Plynlimon (136 miles, if you're fit enough), but even the 18 miles from Monmouth to Chepstow is a richly rewarding hike, with some cracking views along the way – perhaps none better than Wynd Cliff and the breathtaking vista across the giant meander of the river below to Wintour's Leap.

A short jump into Wales proper will find the remarkable Wentwood Forest, hard by the town of Newport. The Woodland Trust is particularly fired up about this wonderful tract of woodland which, at 2,718 acres, is the largest ancient woodland site in Wales. Containing ancient monuments such as Bronze Age barrows and tumuli mentioned in the 12th-century *Book of Llandaff* and once a royal hunting forest, this was clearly a remarkable place with a rich cultural history. In 2005 it looked as if 870 acres of Wentwood would go on the open market, which would most likely have resulted in more of it being clear felled and more conifers planted. The Trust stepped in, and after a massive response to its national appeal was able to purchase the woodland at the turn of the year.

Suddenly the future looks a lot brighter for Wentwood. Although much of the woodland is currently dominated by conifers, flowers associated with ancient woods, such as bluebell, wild daffodil and wood anemone are still very much in evidence. A long-term plan has been devised to return the majority of Wentwood back to broadleaf, thus providing the very best habitat for some of its rarest species such as otters, dormice and pearl-bordered fritillary butterfly, and ensuring that the distinctive calls of the nightjar, woodcock and spotted flycatcher return each spring.

On its western boundary Wentwood overlooks the lower Usk valley, and woodland exploration further up the course of the river, around the towns of Abergavenny and Crickhowell, reveals some beautiful and very individual woods. Within the deep gorge at Cwm Clydach, above Gilwern, is a beech wood growing over the signs of long forgotten iron-making which began here 300 years ago. Look out for the strange bird's-nest orchid, a remarkable little brownish plant that has no chlorophyll, for it takes its sustenance from the leaf litter in which it grows. The name derives from the matted cluster of roots that resemble a bird's nest.

Above Crickhowell an altogether different wood clings to the limestone crags of Craig y Cilau. An early morning walk along the tops is a truly elevating experience, with stunning views of the Usk valley and the Brecon Beacons beyond. Scan the skies above for hunting peregrine falcons, which usually nest here.

Below, the great sweep of the crags, once extensively mined for limestone but now a National Nature Reserve, is a giant rock garden rich with rowan, ash, large-leaved lime and a very rare whitebeam (found only here), which cling precariously to the precipitous cliffs. Along the top path discover amazing little bonsai forms of hawthorn – ancient, tiny specimens that have been continually grazed by sheep and blasted by storms. This is a glorious place, but don't get too carried away and always watch your step.

If you're after something a little more down to earth, and a suitable place to let the kids loose, then head for Cwmcarn Forest Drive. This Forestry Commission wooded park has lots to see and do; whether it's simply having a walk, discovering the amazing giant wood sculptures, or burning it up round the new mountain-biking trail. After your exertions there are plenty of places to picnic or barbecue, and you could even stay over on the excellent camp and caravan site. A whole range of seasonal events linked to sports, crafts and wildlife are also on offer.

The southeast corner of Wales has a fascinating collection of woods to explore, many of which have survived the rigours of several hundred years of coal mining and iron making, which were once the lifeblood of the region. A popular misconception has been that industry destroys woodland, but this was far from the truth. Coal mining needed pit-props and the iron industry once needed vast quantities of charcoal to heat its forges, so well-managed coppice woods were vital for these needs. Only 2.5 miles from Ebbw Vale, a name so redolent of the mining tradition, lies the Silent Valley Local Nature Reserve, perhaps a strangely prophetic name in the wake of so much industrial demise. A mixture of woods, wet flushes and old meadows make this site well worthy of its SSSI status, and much evidence of the industrial heritage of the region can still be discerned here. This is the most westerly and the highest of the native beech woods in Britain. Here the Gwent Wildlife Trust has made a huge effort to involve the local community as part of an ongoing management and conservation partnership, encouraging local people to enjoy their wood, to learn about the wildlife and play an active role in management practice. Surely this is the way forward with woods – what people come to understand and appreciate they will then take the trouble to look after. Soapbox moment over!

If Cwmcarn is a great recreational facility for Newport, Cardiff and the Valleys, then Afan Forest Park is a splendid equivalent for the good people of Neath and Port Talbot. The local name is 'Little Switzerland', and in an area of over 9,000 acres it's almost as big as a little country. Enjoy a host of different walks here, with great opportunities to take in some of the region's cultural and industrial heritage, including evidence of Bronze Age settlements, abandoned mines, tramways and railways, an old canal and even, amid the goodly mix of conifers and broadleaves, some pretty fine wildlife too. Hoards of mountain bikers regularly make a beeline for Afan, as there is now one of the top ten mountain-bike tracks in the world here, with gripping names to the various trails like Hidden Valley, Dead Sheep Gully, Sidewinder and Desolation.

The upper valleys of the rivers Nedd and Mellte contain some of the very best examples of British gorge woodlands, but one of the most dramatic, particularly after a spell of wet weather, is the National Trust's Henrhyd Falls, near Coelbren to the northeast of Neath. Here the river Llech tumbles 27 metres into the deep

Henrhyd Falls

wooded ravine below, making it the highest single drop falls in south Wales. If you're brave enough, take a walk behind the waterfall. If its the salt spray that you seek then head for Gower. Long treasured as a local bolt hole by the city folks of Swansea, the peninsula has some splendid beaches and wonderful wildlife, including the National Nature Reserve at Oxwich Bay, which sits snugly between Oxwich and Nicolaston Woods. With both AONB and SSSI status, this 25-acre site contains a fantastic diversity of habitats, including sand dunes, rocky shoreline, meadows, marshes, streams, reedbeds and heathland; whilst the woods are principally

Nicolaston Woods

of oak, sycamore and hazel, with a scattering of wind-blown, gnarled and twisted conifers.

Further to the west and a grand day out is to be had exploring the verdant valley of the river Gwaun as it flows to the sea at Fishguard. Set in the Pembrokeshire National Park, this is one of the most extensive continuous stretches of semi-natural broadleaved woodland in the southwest of Wales. As might be expected, the dominant species is very much oak, but sycamore, ash, birch and beech feature too, along with planted conifers. In the upper reaches of the valley, at Coed Cilgelynnen, the land has been abandoned by farmers and is mainly a wilderness of raised peat bog dominated by willow and alder, known as Esgyrn Bottom. A little to the north lies Pengelli Forest, which is yet another fine wood, predominantly oak coppice, bisected by numerous streams and with impressive arrays of wild flowers, including dense carpets of the pretty little yellow cow-wheat and a clearing where you may be drowned by the intoxicating sight and scent of the bluebells.

Not far from Devil's Bridge lies the Hafod Estate, once the home of Thomas Johnes, universally accorded the title of Wales'

Ynys-Hir

greatest tree planter. Between 1782 and 1816 he planted no fewer than five million trees over roughly 1,200 acres, much of it difficult upland sites. Today the estate is less than half this size, but much restoration work has been taking place in recent years to bring the beautiful gardens and walks, which Johnes designed for his guests to enjoy 200 years ago, back to something like their original glory. Some of the broadleaf trees which he planted, including outstanding beech, have now matured into stupendous trees.

If it's birding or twitching that you're after then head north to the Dyfi estuary and the wonderful RSPB reserve at Ynys-Hir, where the lowland mixed broadleaf woods, grassland and reedbeds bordering the southern margin of the river harbour all manner of special wildlife. An amazing 32 species of butterfly have been recorded here. The peat bog is home to sundews, bog asphodel, royal fern and rare bog rosemary. Oh yes, and the birds. How about buzzards, peregrines and, one of Wales and the west's great success stories, the red kite? The saltmarshes are preferred by breeding and wintering redshanks and lapwings. Also look for white-fronted geese working the foreshore.

Another hop north to the Mawddach estuary and you can take in yet another RSPB site. At Penmaenpool, watch for the old timber toll bridge (which clatters like mad as you drive over – just a tad concerning). Stay on the south side of the river, trying to ignore the delights of a wholesome lunch and a delicious pint of ale at the George III Hotel, and make your way up into the steep sessile oak woods. A tumbling stream gurgles and splashes its way down as you struggle up the trail, past ancient mossy stone walls and the remains of old goldminers' buildings. Attaining the summit is worth all the hard work, with magnificent views out across the estuary. Pause to draw breath; then that thought of a ploughman's lunch and a chilled pint seems even more appealing.

Look on the map and you'll see a huge splodge of green to the north of Dolgellau. Taking in the valleys of the Mawddach, Eden, Wen and Gain are 9,000 acres of the Forestry Commission's Coed y Brenin Forest Park. This is, quite unashamedly, conifer territory; impressive plantations of Douglas fir, Scots pine and larch predominate, but here and there broadleaf woodland rings the changes, particularly along the rivers. This is commercial forestry in all its vastness, but the Forestry Commission is deeply committed to also making Coed y Brenin one of the very best amenity forests in Britain. A brand new visitor centre will act as a focal point for a variety of leisure pursuits and an information hub and exhibition centre for the park's landscape and wildlife attributes. If you're quiet you may catch a glimpse of a fallow deer deep in one of the remote glades and you'll certainly come across the massive wood ant 'citadels'. Mosses, liverworts, ferns and lichens abound here, and birders will be keen to spot crossbill, goldcrest and goshawk amongst the conifers, as well as black grouse or the tiny merlin on the heather moorland. There are remnants of old gold mines and copper mines to be found, trails to walk, courses to orienteer, tracks to mountain bike and play areas to exhaust the kids.

The distant peaks of Snowdonia beckon and, set about one of Britain's greatest centres for mountain activities, some of the finest tracts of ancient oakwood in Wales, if not the whole of Britain. The Vales of Ffestiniog and Maentwrog, and the Artro valley below the Rhinog hills, are all most splendidly wooded with ancient oaks, most of which were once coppiced, but over the last century have been allowed to do their own thing. The year-round humidity, a result (dare we say it) of the plentiful rainfall and mild temperatures here, has created exactly the right conditions for a host of rare and beautiful ferns, lichens, mosses and liverworts. These 'Atlantic' oakwoods have been sought out by enthusiastic naturalists and lovers of romantic scenery for more than 200 years. The Maentwrog Woods are a whole collection of sites with slightly different characters, some with planted conifers mixed in, but for a taste of the true 'Atlantics' try Coed Llyn Mair with its gurgling mountain streams, mossy boulders and lichen–clad twisted oaks.

One of the delights of the north coast of Wales is the Aber Valley in the foothills of the Carneddau mountains, between Bangor and Conwy. A walk into the valley takes in a wide variety of habitats, along the course of one of the steepest river valleys in England and Wales, with the goal of the dramatic waterfall of Rhaeadr Fawr. On the east side of the valley planted conifers dominate, but opposite, on the steep rocky slopes, ancient sessile oakwoods still thrive. The wetter parts of the valley bottom are mainly alder and willow, much of which has undergone a revived coppicing regime. A phenomenal diversity of plant and birdlife abounds and, as you climb higher, you'll come under the watchful gaze of rugged little mountain ponies, once bred for use as pit ponies in the mines, but now completely wild. A tour of Wales wouldn't be complete without mention of two of its greatest stretches of inland water and their accompanying attractions, both set in the mighty county of Powys. At the northern extremity lies Lake Vyrnwy, a vast manmade lake built as a reservoir in the 1880s in order to provide water for the city of Liverpool. Four-and-a-half miles long and half-a-mile wide the Lake Vyrnwy Estate covers more than 24,000 acres, owned by Severn Trent Water. It is also an RSPB nature reserve. This is a carefully managed landscape, which aims to maximise financial, environmental and social benefits. Successful moorland management has provided a mosaic of habitats for rare wildlife and the broadleaf woods, principally of sessile oak, are being expanded to encourage yet more species. The conifer population can boast the tallest Douglas fir in the whole of Wales, at an awesome 205 feet. There's a super sculpture trail here and during the summer months local artist and carver, Andy Hancock, runs green woodworking courses. You can sail or canoe, cycle or hop on a horse and, apparently, there's plenty of good fishing to be had. Of course there are lots of trails to walk and soon, if you're feeling really energetic, there will be a 12-mile circular walk around the whole lake.

Further to the south, in the hills above the small market town of Rhayader, lies the reservoir lake system of the Elan valley, with its monolithic stone dams built at the turn of the nineteenth century to ensure a reliable source of water for the city of Birmingham. Building work on the different phases of the damming system progressed for more than half a century, and the final part, the Claerwen dam, wasn't opened until 1952. Today Welsh Water is actively involved in enhancing the biodiversity of the woodland around the lakes to encourage more species of wildlife and, as they are harvested, many of the conifer stands will be replaced by broadleaf species. Again oak predominates here, and supports a fine collection of mosses, lichens, ferns and fungi. The species tally for Elan is impressive – more than 300 species of flowering plant (including eight different orchids), 27 species of butterfly and more than 200 species of moth. Add to this the very likely chance that you will spot several red kites soaring above, for this is one of their Welsh strongholds. An Elan Valley Trail and excellent visitor centre with all the facilities you'd expect, plus a busy schedule of a huge variety of special events throughout the year with such enticing titles as Bug Bonanza, Dambusters Walk, Mammal Masks and Animal Tasks and (who could forget) National Bog Day.

This whistle-stop tour around just a few of the wonderful woods, both great and small, to be found throughout the length and breadth of Wales barely scratches the surface, but should whet your appetite for some serious woodland exploring. Whether you're a nature buff, a casual stroller or someone who wants to get out and get mucky on a bike you'll find the wood to suit you in this book. So, what are you waiting for? Get your boots on and go . . .

ARCHIE MILES

MAP 1

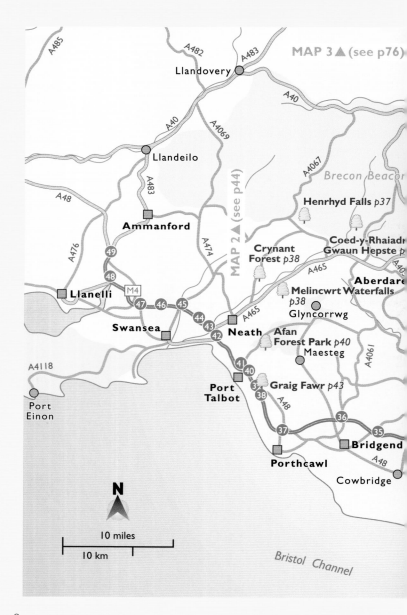

MAP 3 ▲ (see p76)

Llandovery

Llandeilo

MAP 2 ▲ (see p44)

Brecon Beacor

Henrhyd Falls p37

Ammanford

Crynant
Forest p38

Coed-y-Rhaiadr
Gwaun Hepste p

Aberdare

Melincwrt Waterfalls
p38

Glyncorrwg

Llanelli

49

48

M4

47 46 45

44

43

42

Swansea

Neath

Afan
Forest Park p40

Maesteg

41

40

3

38

Graig Fawr p43

**Port
Talbot**

Port
Einon

37

36

35

Bridgend

Porthcawl

Cowbridge

N

10 miles

10 km

Bristol Channel

18

Hereford

A470

Brecon

Pwyll y Wrach p34

A479

A465

A49

Talybont &
Taf Fechan
Forests p34

Coed y Cerrig Mynydd Du &
Strawberry Cottage Wood p32

Ross-on-Wye

A40

Crickhowell

Coed Cefn p32

A466

Abergavenny

Priory Grove p20

Monmouth

erthyr
ydfil

Ebbw
Vale

Brynmawr

The Punchbowl
p31

A40

Beaulieu
Wood
p20

Wye Valley
Woodland
p22

Rhymney

Blaenavon

A467

Silent Valley
p30

Priory
Wood
p30

Croes
Robert
Wood p21

Tintern
Wood
p24

wm Darran
ountry Park
ountain
Ash

Pontypool

A449

Bargoed

Cwmbran

Cwmcarn Forest p28

Wentwood
p25

Chepstow

St Pierre
Great
Wood
p24

ntypridd

Sirhowy
Country
Park p27

Risca

Penhow
Woodlands
p26

A48

M48

A470

Caerphilly
Woods
p26

26 — 25

24

23a 23

22

Caerphilly

M4

30

29

Newport

Caldicot

M4

1

A473

32

29a

River Severn

M49

17

34

33

18a

18

CARDIFF

19

M5

BRISTOL

Barry

20

A370

Weston-
super-Mare

21

A38

19

MAP 1

Priory Grove
Monmouth

On A4136 at Monmouth, head southeast, then take Hadnock road northeast until wood appears on the right. There are two laybys for parking. (SO526139)
32 ha (79 acres) AONB SSSI
Woodland Trust

Lying on a steep-sided hill, Priory Grove forms part of a striking landscape and was once a crucial part of the British charcoal-making industry.

Evidence can still be found today, with several flattened, blackened areas of the forest floor visible amongst the semi-natural woodland.

The wood is made up of oak, beech, ash and birch with wild cherry, small-leaved lime, hazel, willow and aspen also present along with planted sweet chestnut and larch.

Popular with local residents, the woods lie close to an A road and the noise of the traffic is present on much of an otherwise pleasant walk through the site.

It's a short but sharp climb up into the wood from the main entrance. As the ride opens out there is lush vegetation consisting of ferns, woodrush, brambles and spurge while, in the shade of the beech, you can spot hart's-tongue fern.

Pedestrian access is via a network of public and permissive footpaths.

Beaulieu Wood
Monmouth

From Monmouth, take A4136 east. The National Trust's The Kymin is signed from the road. Follow the lane up, and park in The Kymin car park. Beaulieu Wood is to the north of The Kymin. (SO528128)
17 ha (42 acres) AONB
Woodland Trust

This historic ancient woodland site is prominently set overlooking the River Wye and Monmouth, and part of the Wye Valley Area of Outstanding Natural Beauty.

Much of the site was replanted with conifer stands in the 1950s and 60s, and a largely closed canopy leaves little growing on the woodland floor, other than scattered rowan and holly.

Where the canopy is more open, along the eastern ridge, for example, where mature semi-natural woodland remains intact with mature beech and oak, you can find bracken, broad-buckler, fern, bramble and bilberry.

Along the northern margin is a fringe of more varied semi-natural woodland, with a blend of ash, oak, wild cherry, silver birch, goat willow and hazel. Several southern wood ant nests have been recorded.

The site has a dark, 'fantasy' feel, with a path wending through large moss-clad boulders, with ferns and twisted, gnarled birch and beech trees.

Croes Robert Wood
Monmouth

Leave Monmouth on B4293 travelling towards Trellech. Turn right past Trellech School signposted Cwmcarvan. After 1.5km (1 mile) take first right turn. Reserve entrance and car park on right. (SO475060) 14 ha (35 acres) AONB SSSI

Gwent Wildlife Trust

Well-loved and traditionally managed, this ancient woodland site is a delightful place to visit, particularly if you are looking to 'get away from it all'.

Lying in the Wye Valley Area of Outstanding Natural Beauty, the wood is home to many mammals, including the endangered dormouse, weasel, fallow deer and badger.

Although small, the site is well signed and covered by a circular walk along good rides through a broadleaf-dominated landscape of coppiced sycamore, hazel and ash.

Coppicing work and charcoal burning, which continue today, offer the visitor the chance to see how broadleaved woodland is traditionally managed.

There is a lush ground flora, with tall ferns, greater woodrush, foxglove, bluebells and meadowsweet to name a few. And the presence of several springs and wet flushes add to the diversity of the woodland population.

Autumn visitors will unveil a feast of fungi including King Alfred's Cakes, coral spot fungus, candle snuff fungus and The Goblet.

MAP 1

Wye Valley Woods
Chepstow - Monmouth

Located to the west of the A466. (SO529059)
AONB, SSSI

Various including Forestry Commission

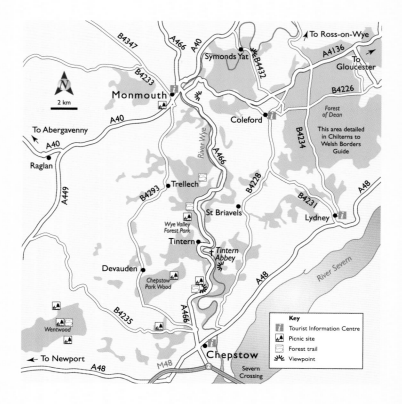

For sheer size, beauty and conservation value, the Wye Valley Woodlands score as one of the most important sites in the UK.

Even a full day would not do the valley justice – you need at least a weekend to appreciate the wealth of sights and sounds.

A good starting point is the Wye Valley walk, a stunning 136-mile trail following the river valley from Chepstow to the slopes of Plynlimon, criss-crossing the border between England and Wales.

The Wye has been hailed as Britain's most unspoilt river and there is a rich variety of woods to enjoy along its course. Some of the walking is tough going but the reward is breathtaking scenery, rich in history.

Woodland covers nearly a third of the Wye Valley Area of Outstanding Natural Beauty – and has been identified as one of the country's most important woodland conservation sites.

The Lower Wye Valley's native woods are cited as some of the best examples of ravine woodland surviving in Europe and are designated a special area of conservation.

Semi-natural woodland covers an almost continuous 18-mile run of the Wye gorge, with ash-dominated ravine woodland and an intimate mix of other woods including beech, yew and oak.

Little wonder that some nationally important species – such as greater and lesser horseshoe bats, dormice, white admiral butterflies, Tintern spurge and the narrow-leaved bitter cress can be found here.

The woods are being managed to encourage natural species in an effort to counterbalance the extensive conifer plantations that replaced much of the original ancient coppices.

See entries for Tintern (p24), Beaulieu and Priory Grove (p20). The Exploring Woodland Guide *Chilterns to the Welsh Borders* contains sites on the England side of the Wye Valley.

MAP 1

Tintern Wood
Trellech

From Tintern follow signs for Catbrook and Trellech at junction adjacent to the Wye Valley Hotel and follow for 4km (2.5 miles). At junction entrance to Whitestone car park opposite (SO525030) 600 ha (1483 acres) AONB
Forestry Commission

There are four main approaches to Tintern Wood – Manor Wood, Whitestone, the Tintern Trail and Upper Wyndcliff – each one providing a different experience.

Enter via Whitestone for some good family facilities, including children's play equipment. The woods stand on fertile ground over 600ft above the Wye, and include oak, beech, Norway spruce and grand fir.

The rim of the valley here provides magnificent views across the river and a path north offers some worthwhile vantage points. The Wye Valley Walk runs through the site and another, the Tall Trees Walk, leads through a cathedral-like grove of Douglas firs.

Much of Bargain Wood is now beech, though the site was once coppice oak, while few of the woods in the lower Wye Valley are natural, apart from odd semi-natural fragments.

The Tintern Trail gives you the chance to explore the woods of the Angidy Valley.

Exploration is on forest tracks with some challenging rougher sections.

St Pierre Great Wood
Shirenewton

From M48, take A466 north, then A48 southwest. Turn right to Shirenewton. Wood on left, with car park at northern most tip of wood. (ST503932) 367Ha (907 acres)
Forestry Commission

There is a pleasant feel to this well-managed, mixed-age beech woodland, which is popular with locals.

There are lots of well-maintained forest tracks and footpaths to help you explore, with the chance to glimpse the surrounding countryside of open fields and hedgerows.

There is good regeneration of

trees and you will spot ash, hazel, elder, oak and small-leaved lime with intermittent conifers, while scattered yew and holly create the understorey. Sedges, bramble and silverweed can be found occasionally on the woodland floor.

The edges of the ride are verdant, with swathes of tall herbs such as willow herb, wood spurge and vervain, while honeysuckle and old man's beard hang down in coils and ropes.

You can extend your day out with a visit to Chepstow Park Wood and Fedw to the north, a vast forest of conifers with many mature areas, and further still the Forestry Commission's Ravensnest Buckle.

Wentwood
Newport

Take A48 from Newport. Look out for right turn to Park Seymour. Follow road carefully through small village and up hillside to main block of woodland, where there are several pull-ins, a car park and picnic area. (ST412939) 352ha (870 acres)
Various including Woodland Trust & Forest Commission

At first sight Wentwood, Wales' largest planted ancient woodland, looks little more than a typical conifer plantation.

But look closer and you discover veteran beech, oak, sweet chestnut and ash, not to mention a roe deer or two.

Exceptionally good access is provided in the form of several well-made forest tracks that follow the undulations of the forest like an American highway. Smaller paths branch off to reveal centuries-old ways through what was once a broadleaf forest. Opportunities will be developed for waymarked paths in the future. Look out also for ancient monuments, tumuli and other earthworks.

Where beech woods remain, carpets of bluebells proliferate in spring. Look out too for veteran beech pollards which often follow old boundaries.

In cleared sections you can find foxgloves and other wildflowers in abundance. There are also wetland areas and a pond with dragonflies and damselflies darting about.

MAP 1

Penhow Woods
Newport

From J23 of M4, follow sign to Magor back under motorway. Take minor road to Penhow. Parking for one car as you approach wood on right. (ST417900)

19ha (40 acres) SSSI

Countryside Council for Wales

While Penhow National Nature Reserve is made up of three woods, Coed Wen is the only one which offers public access. Set within farmland today, old maps show the wood at twice its size around 150 years ago.

Deep and fertile soils here support tall ash trees, festooned with long, hanging honeysuckle, ivy and old man's beard. There are large oaks dating back to the turn of the 19th century. Look for giant stumps of ash and elm which indicate earlier management of this wood through coppicing.

Growing beneath them is a rich floral mix of bluebell, wild daffodil, lesser periwinkle, dog's mercury, enchanter's nightshade, wood anemone, and hart's-tongue fern. And look out too for the rarer sight of upright spurge, green hellebore and bird's nest orchid.

Caerphilly Woods
Caerphilly

From Junction 28 of M4 take A468 to Caerphilly and left towards Draethen. Go through Draethen to the Maenllwyd Inn and either of the three nearby car parks. (ST206867, ST201853, ST172864).523Ha (1293 acres)

Forestry Commission

Part of a rolling landscape of imposing hills, hedgerows and mature trees, this is a pleasant place in which to get away from it all.

The woodland offers a good balance of coniferous and deciduous trees. And while there is not much in the way of flora on the forest floor, there is a lot of regenerating ash, beech and sycamore to enjoy.

The forest grows around the Caerphilly Mountain Ridge, and as the forest opens up, there is a good view of the surrounding landscape. Beside one site is a huge, disused quarry as well as remnants of former industrial workings elsewhere.

Sections of the site include ash, oak and beech, which can be explored from a good variety of bridleways, tracks and footpaths. Several areas beside the track are swathed with buddleia and Himalayan balsam.

Sirhowy Country Park
Abercarn

Turn left off A467, northwest of Newport, at roundabout when dual carriageway ends. (ST210912) 405ha (1000 acres) SSSI

Caerphilly County Borough Council

Sirhowy Country Park

Well managed, suitable for all and a pleasure to visit, this wonderful site has everything from pleasant strolls to more challenging hillside climbs.

A ranger base at Sirhowy offers plenty of information about the site and its well-mapped trails.

The forest road and track follows the River Sirhowy and footpaths lead through tall, graceful western hemlock up the steep hillside. For those willing to tackle the ankle-twisting path there are beautiful hues to enjoy in the velvety textured undergrowth of moss and fern.

Higher up is a lush oak woodland, carpeted with bluebells in spring. From here you can enjoy pleasant valley views including rows of miners' cottages – a reminder of the area's heritage.

On the hilltop are two Bronze Age burial mounds and on a clear day you can see clear across the Brecon Beacons, Severn Estuary, Caerphilly Castle and the spectacular Sirhowy and Rhymney valleys.

27

Cwmcarn Forest

Cwmcarn Forest
Abercarn

Take J28 from M4 towards Risca, driving north for 11km (7 miles) on A467. Follow brown tourist signs off this road. (ST220946) 1315 ha (3249 acres)

Forestry Commission & Caerphilly County Borough Council

Allow a full day to visit this fantastic, magical forest – or better still, take a tent or caravan and make a weekend of it.

Take one of two cycle trails or enjoy a seven-mile drive through the site. For children there is a numeracy trail and there are lots of picnic, barbecue and parking sites with a variety of exciting themes.

One highlight is the giant's court, with wood carvings based on tales from the Mabinogion, and a magical storytelling amphitheatre. Another has a North American theme, with colourful hilltop totem poles.

The forest is grand, lush and rich in endless shades of green with moss and ferns lining the floor and gracefully drooping conifer branches lining the road. Travel higher up for stunning views of the surrounding landscape and Severn Estuary.

There are endless things to do, from mountain-bike tracks and guided walks, play areas, interpretive boards outlining the industrial past, and an Iron Age fort.

There is an entrance charge for the Forest Drive.

Cwm Darran Country Park

Cwm Darran Country Park
Bargoed

On A469, 3km (2 miles) north of Bargoed, take turning to Deri and follow signs. (SO118034)

75 ha (185 acres)

Caerphilly County Borough Council

Nature is reclaiming its sovereignty over a site which for years was given over to the mining industry.

Some 15,000 trees were planted in 1979 when Ogilvie Colliery closed and the result has been the creation of a wonderfully peaceful country park, complete with woodland walks, playground, cycle trails – including one converted from a former railway line – and links to longer footpaths through the Upper Rhymney Valley.

A central feature of the site is the manmade Ogilvie lake, which is a focus for fishing and wildlife. A Tarmac path around the lake leads on to four waymarked routes through attractive, undulating countryside.

A stream runs down the centre of the valley, with open grassland and shrubs on the valley bottom. The woods line the west-facing valley slopes. There are areas of open grassland and meadows.

Clear way marking and several self-guided walk leaflets aid the visitor.

MAP 1

Silent Valley
Ebbw Vale

On A4046 4km (2.5 miles) south of
Ebbw Vale. Leave the one-way
system in Cwm on the northern
side, turning second right at a
brown tourist sign. Car park 400m
by Cwm Cemetery. Walk
northwards across flat grass playing
area and along path to entrance.
(SO187062) 50 ha (124 acres) SSSI
Gwent Wildlife Trust

Nature is fighting back in this
well-loved community
woodland which boasts
Britain's highest beech woods.
  Flanked on one site by a
former mining village, much of
Silent Valley is designated a Site
of Special Scientific Interest
(SSSI) and some trees are more
than 300 years old.

The site is composed of two
ancient semi-natural beech
woodlands, one of the most
westerly in Europe. The woods
are interspersed with wet
flushes and open areas, once
part of medieval farms.
  The valley has felt the impact
of both the coal mining and
steel industries but today the
presence of bearded lichens
bears testimony to the purity
of the air.
  Birdlife thrives with robins,
wrens, redstarts and pied
flycatchers nesting on the
reserve, which is also home for
insects, bats and butterflies,
including the small pearl-
bordered fritillary.
  The mining spoil has been
colonised by mosses and
liverworts and in wetter areas
alder trees provide valuable food
for siskins, redpolls and tits.

Priory Wood
Abergavenny

From Abergavenny take B4598 south
towards Usk. Turn left immediately
after crossing River Usk up a minor
road. Wood is on right after 800m.
(SO352058) 5ha (12 acres) SSSI
Gwent Wildlife Trust

Towering, ivy-clad cherry trees
provide a striking sight for
visitors to this interesting wood.
The prominent, ridged bark of
the trees is a particularly
beautiful feature.
  Sound is also significant in the
wood, which is rich in birdlife
from pied flycatcher and great
spotted woodpecker to

hawfinch, which sometimes breeds here. At the hill-top nest boxes are located on trees and if quiet, it's possible to glimpse a blackcap or nuthatch.

A circular path takes you through this varied broadleaf site of wild cherry, beech, oak, ash, birch and yew. There are dense thickets of bramble, with hawthorn, hazel and long ropes of honeysuckle and ivy providing good cover for birds and small mammals.

In spring bluebells and dog's mercury bloom and in summer, the enchanter's nightshade thrives among moss carpets. Noctule bats can be seen on an evening hunt for food.

Visit in the autumn and it's a great place for fungi, with species including the magpie inkcaps.

The Punchbowl
Abergavenny

From Abergavenny take A465 west, then B4246 south. Follow minor road until entrance to site on left. (SO281111) 38 ha (93 acres)
Woodland Trust

Peaceful, breathtakingly beautiful and physically challenging, this is a truly magical site.

Towering ancient beeches stand on steep hillsides surround a calm lake, with birds singing in the woods while the visitor drinks in magnificent views across the River Usk.

The wooded slopes form some of the highest altitude ancient semi-natural woodland in Britain.

Once part of the 16th-century charcoal industry and the 19th-century coal industry, the Punchbowl boasts some beech trees that date back to the 17th century.

Dense shade cast by the imposing beech trees means that flora on the site is limited. But there is much life here in the shape of insects, buzzards, green woodpeckers, tawny owls and bats.

Public access follows a bridleway, a sunken lane and permissive paths with several viewpoints within the site giving views of the dramatic Usk Valley landscape.

The site includes wood pasture that provides important areas of grazing for sheep, so you are asked to keep dogs under strict control.

MAP 1

Coed Cefn
Crickhowell
Follow minor road east of
Crickhowell, on northern side of
A40. As the road climbs, giving
excellent views back over the
town, wood is on left. (SO226185)
11 ha (27 acres)
Woodland Trust

An Iron Age hill fort – now a
scheduled ancient monument –
lies at the heart of the
woodland, atop a gentle hill
overlooking Crickhowell.

It's explored via an easy
circular path, the first section
of which takes you past some
recently planted oak and ash

trees which replaced spruce as
part of a plan to restore the site
to its ancient woodland
character.

Coed Cefn consists mainly of
oak, beech and Norway spruce
which was planted in 1958. Its
southern section is dominated
by self-sown ash while the
western tail of the wood has
semi-mature oak and
sycamore, under-planted in
places with Grand fir.

There is very little shrub
layer, the woodland floor being
dominated by bramble and
bluebell which transforms each
spring into a carpet of blue.

From here you can enjoy
views of the heather-covered
hills and pasture beyond.

Coed y Cerrig, Mynydd Du, Strawberry Cottage Wood
Abergavenny
From Abergavenny follow A465
north for 6.5km (4 miles). Left at
Llanvihangel Crucorney, following
signs toward Llanthony Abbey. At
Stanton turn left and follow Forest
Coal Pit signs. Coed y Cerrig is
either side of road, car park on right.
Mynydd Du 6.5km (4 miles) further
along road. For Strawberry Cottage
Wood turn right in Stanton after

pub, down steep hill to river. Park by
footbridge and follow public
footpath sign through fields.
(Coed-y-Cerrig SO292211, 12 ha
(30 acres)), (Mynydd Du SO262258,
1100 ha (2718 acres)), (Strawberry
Cottage Wood SO312215, 6ha (15
acres)) AONB, SSSI
**Countryside Council for Wales,
Forestry Commission, Gwent
Wildlife Trust**

Mynydd Du

Hidden away in a valley against the giant backdrop of the Black Mountains, Coed y Cerrig National Nature Reserve is a beautiful site.

The wood is bisected by a narrow lane, with wet alder woodland to one side. Thanks to an accessible boardwalk, the route can be enjoyed by all.

Higher up the ground is drier and ash and birch dominate the scenery, while at the top there is a flat plateau, rich in fungi, where larger oak, ash and beech trees thrive.

Neighbouring Mynydd Du lies on the southern sides of the mountains and this once-populated area is now a wonderful mature, dark, majestic forest. Higher up the gently climbing valley is deciduous woodland, with lovely, varied views.

Completing the trio, Strawberry Cottage Wood is a pleasant hillside sessile oak and hazel wood with interesting plants including nettle-leaved bellflower and loose-spiked wood sedge. Look out for redstarts, pied flycatchers and the lesser-spotted woodpecker.

33

MAP 1

Pwyll y Wrach
Talgarth

Follow A479 south from the main square in Talgarth and fork left almost immediately into Pendent Road. Continue over river and up hill past hospital, following narrow lane until reserve entrance on right. (SO165326)
8.5 ha (21 acres) SSSI
Brecknock Wildlife Trust

This delightful oak-ash woodland, one of Wales' most important, is a site for all seasons.

Rich in history, flora, wildlife and botanical interest, it boasts tutsan and toothwort and reaches peak beauty in spring with its bounty of bluebell, early-purple orchid, wood anemone and lesser celandine.

Tawny owls, jays and many other bird species frequent the canopy and this is the best site in Brecknock for dormice.

Sessile oaks grow on the site's upper soils, with heather and hard fern, while lower down the valley side are ash trees and lime-loving shrubs such as spindle and dogwood. Butterflies abound in sunny glades and in the woods are woodpeckers and pied flycatchers. Dippers and grey wagtail – and the odd otter – might be spotted by the stream.

Visitors can enjoy a specially constructed easy access trail from the entrance to the heart of the reserve and an exciting geological trail explores the events of 400 million years ago – leaflet available from Trust office.

Talybont & Taf Fechan Forests
Talybont-on-Usk

Turn off A40 between Brecon and Bwlch following signs for Talybont-on-Usk. Once in Talybont follow signs for Talybont reservoir. Passing through Aber, look for Forestry Commission signs. Continue through Talybont Forest for Taf Fechan Forest.

(Talybont SO099196),
(Taf Fechan SO042163)
1929 ha (4,766 acres) AONB
Forestry Commission

Traditional forestry plantation on a grand scale – that sums up Talybont and Taf Fechan Forests.

Taf Fechan Forest

Separate, yet linked, both sites are incredibly atmospheric and popular with the people of South Wales.

One of the best ways to get an overall view is to drive, drinking in the vast swathes of conifers that clad the mountainsides. Cycling and walking are also good ways of seeing the site, where the autumn browns and yellows of deciduous woodland contrast with the dark greens of serried ranks of conifer nearer the reservoir.

Every turn of the road brings the harsh beauty of the rugged landscape into focus. Talybont, lying alongside Glyn Gollwyn and the Talybont Reservoir, has at its head the waterfalls of Blaen y Glyn and is home to badgers, otters, polecats, hares, foxes and bats as well as buzzards, kestrels, and hobbies. Taf Fechan is a large upland forest and, though popular, boasts secluded picnic spots and resting places.

MAP 1

Coed-y-Rhaiadr/
Gwaun Hepste
Ystradfellte village

Take A4059 north at Hirwaun, then left on minor road to Ystradfellte village. Waterfalls car parks on left. (SN932112)
779 ha (1925 acres) AONB, SSSI
Forestry Commission

Stunning scenery teeming with wildlife and lovely waterfalls and caves, this forest is hugely popular. But great care is needed as the river gorges are dangerously steep and slippery.

Much of the walking is challenging, on roughly made tracks. But there is so much worth seeing, including 600 different plants.

Known as Coed y Rhaiadr –

'wood of the waterfalls' – the site spans the headwaters of the River Neath and the waters of the Mellte, Hepste and Nedd Fechan have cut deep gorges and caverns into the limestone and created waterfalls and ravines downstream.

Here, beneath a dense canopy of oaks, more than 230 species of moss and fern thrive – among them many rare ones. There are several waterfall walks, including a 400 metre all-ability trail leading to the Sychryd cascades, a four-mile linear walk and the Four Falls Trail leading to four spectacular waterfalls.

Visitors are asked to keep away from the old mine workings.

Gwaun Hepste

Henrhyd Falls
Coelbren

From Abercraf take A4221 to
village of Coelbren. Henrhyd Falls
signed from this road. For car
parking, go through village, left at T
junction and over bridge. Car park
on left after 100m. (SN854122)
11 ha (26 acres) SSSI
National Trust

Henrhyd Falls

Lying in 'waterfall country' on
the southern rim of the
Brecon Beacons National Park,
Henrhyd Falls set in the Graig
Llech Gorge is a stunner.

The highest falls in South
Wales, in winter the powerful
river Llech cascades over a 30-
metre-high cliff, assaulting the
senses as soon as you enter
the wood.

A well-made path descends
steeply down from the car
park, through oak woodland
with glimpses of the falls and
river way below. The walk is
challenging – not a good idea
if you suffer from vertigo.

The dense woodland is a far
cry from the boundless open
spaces that fill most of the
national park. The moist
canopy creates a haven for
mosses, liverworts, ferns and
lichens.

The site is home to such
varied birdlife as pied
flycatcher, redstart, wood
warbler, nuthatch, great spotted
woodpecker and kingfisher.

MAP 1

Crynant Forest
Crynant, Dulais Valley

From J43 of M4 take A465 north, then left onto A4109 towards Crynant. Car park on right. (SN789036) 939 ha (2320 acres)
Forestry Commission

A huge plantation with conifers stretching upward almost into the clouds, the massive Crynant Forest in the Dulais Valley is a delightful site where you can walk for miles without meeting another soul.

Part of the area where steel making and the industrial revolution evolved, it is a lovely gateway into the Breacon Beacons National Park.

This is a wonderful resource both for local residents and tourists who flock to the area where coal and iron workings once dominated the economy. The former Cefn Coed Colliery, now museum, near the car park provides some evidence of the area's industrial heritage.

Beyond the Roman road which runs along the ridge of Mynydd Resolfen lies the extensive forests of the Vale of Neath.

The Swansea Bay area also boasts lovely sandy beaches, mountains and rivers with wildlife, so there is always plenty to keep visitors busy.

Melincwrt Falls
Resolven

From Neath take A465 north to Resolven. Entering village on B4434, road bears right. Follow road until car park reached on right. Entrance to wood over road. (SN825017) 5 ha (12 acres)
Wildlife Trust of South and West Wales

An ancient broadleaved woodland, with a stream and waterfall, this delightful little site is well used by local people.

Sessile oak, birch, ash, rowan and cherry populate the wood, while along the valley floor are alder, wych elm and small-leaved lime.

No fewer than 80 species of wildflower and 20 species of fern grow here. Bluebells carpet the woodland floor in spring, while common cow-wheat cloaks the upper slopes in summer, and alternate-leaved golden saxifrage in wetter areas.

And there is plenty of birdlife, including redstart, wood warbler and pied flycatcher while dipper and grey wagtail can be found along the stream.

An 80ft-high waterfall is approached from a well-made path running gradually upward from the stream. It's a one-path route to the falls and takes about 20 minutes to walk there and back. Look out too for the remains of an 18th-century ironworks.

Since Turner painted the falls in 1794 they have continued to inspire artists and poets.

Melincwrt Falls

MAP 1

Afan Forest Park

Swansea

From J40 of M4 take A4107 north. Afan Forest Park is signed. Continue up valley past the Afan Forest Park visitor centre, following signs for Glyncorrwg village. Information centre signed Mountain Bike Centre on left before village. (Afan SS817947) (Glyncorrwg SS873991)

6000Ha (14800 acres)

Forestry Commission

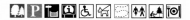

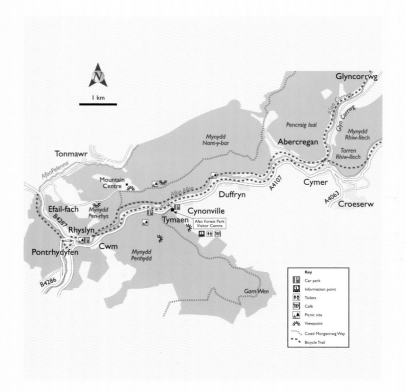

Afan Forest Park

Known locally as 'Little Switzerland', Afan Forest Park must be one of Wales' best-kept secrets.

Voted one of the world's top ten single mountain bike tracks, it is a bikers' Mecca, with challenging trails through such descriptive areas as 'the hidden valley', 'dead sheep gully', 'sidewinder' and 'desolation'.

The narrow valley sides are tree-clad, but the tops are clear allowing wide views of Gower, Exmoor and Brecon Beacons – a far cry from the area's former incarnation as a centre of mining.

The forest is massive but there are lots of stopping places with visitors' centres, museums and cafes, a campsite and shops to cater for a host of needs.

Buzzards circle overhead. As you reach the stream the sound of rushing water takes over from the buzzard's plaintive cry.

Among majestic conifers are areas of deciduous woodland featuring moss-clad ash, birch and oaks. The ground is bedecked with grass, fern and bramble, and bilberry on the higher slopes.

Above Glyncorrwg village, man has again teamed up with

41

MAP 1

nature to create mountain-biking heaven in the shape of a massive mountain forest covering lots of slopes.

The result of a major community project by the villagers, the site is hugely popular and boasts three manmade lakes, an adult education centre, business unit, bike shop and café.

A network of forest tracks enables the visitor to navigate the site and plans are in hand for developing signed walks. There is even a bike lift service to take keen cyclists high up into the forest.

Most of the forest is coniferous while up on the moorland tops is a vast expanse of grass, rush and other moorland species.

Afan Forest Park

Graig Fawr
Port Talbot
Junction 38 on M4. Take A48
signed Margam Country Park. Turn
off to left and pull in by wood,
taking care not to block entrance.
(SS793869) 51 ha (127 acres)

Woodland Trust

Any motorist travelling on the
M4 in this region will have
noticed dramatic Graig Fawr, a
prominent feature of the
south-facing slope nestling
against Margam Country Park.
  Visitors enjoy its atmospheric
mixed canopy of pine, spruce,
beech, sweet chestnut and
other native broadleaf trees.
And the area is renowned for
its population of nesting

kestrel, buzzard, sparrow hawk
and little and tawny owls.
  Much of the site has ancient
origins – evident from the
springtime displays of bluebell,
wood sorrel, primrose and
wood anemone. Prior to
Woodland Trust ownership old
oak trees were felled to make
way for the planting of conifer
and other non-native
broadleaves. Now it is managed
to encourage broadleaf trees
such as ash, oak and sycamore
to flourish.
  The site is also very rich
archaeologically, with a
restored 14th century monks'
bath house, a Second World
War radar station with
wonderful views, and a
Napoleonic look-out camp

MAP 2

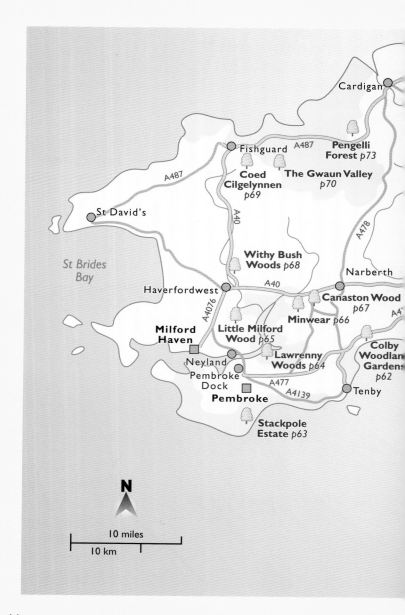

Cardigan

Fishguard A487

**Pengelli
Forest** p73

**Coed
Cilgelynnen**
p69

The Gwaun Valley
p70

A487

St David's

A40

A478

*St Brides
Bay*

**Withy Bush
Woods** p68

A40 Narberth

Haverfordwest

Canaston Wood
p67

A4076

Minwear p66

**Milford
Haven**

**Little Milford
Wood** p65

**Colby
Woodland
Gardens**
p62

Neyland

**Lawrenny
Woods** p64

Pembroke
Dock A477

A4139

Tenby

Pembroke

**Stackpole
Estate** p63

N

10 miles

10 km

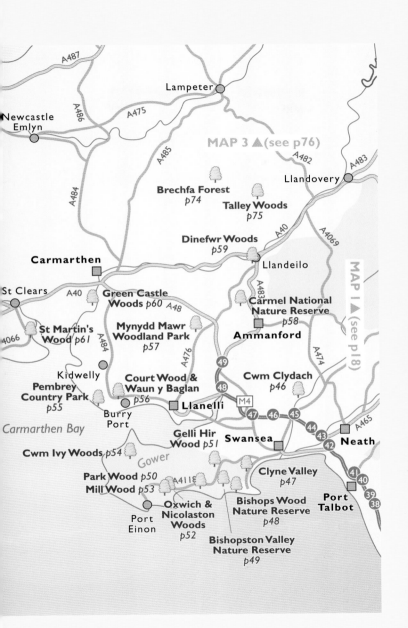

A487

Lampeter

A486

A475

Newcastle
Emlyn

MAP 3 ▲ (see p76)

A485

A482

A483

Llandovery

Brechfa Forest
p74

Talley Woods
p75

A484

A40

A4069

Dinefwr Woods
p59

Carmarthen

Llandeilo

St Clears

A40

Green Castle
Woods *p60* A48

Carmel National
Nature Reserve
p58

A4066

St Martin's
Wood *p61*

Mynydd Mawr
Woodland Park
p57

A4833

MAP 1 ▲ (see p18)

Ammanford

A476

Kidwelly

Pembrey
Country Park
p55

Court Wood &
Waun y Baglan
p56

Burry
Port

Llanelli

M4

49

48

Cwm Clydach
p46

A474

47 46 45

44

A465

43

42

Neath

Carmarthen Bay

Cwm Ivy Woods *p54*

Gelli Hir
Wood *p51*

Swansea

Gower

Park Wood *p50*
Mill Wood *p53*

A4118

Clyne Valley
p47

41 40

Port
Einon

Oxwich &
Nicolaston
Woods
p52

Bishops Wood
Nature Reserve
p48

Port
Talbot

39
38

Bishopston Valley
Nature Reserve
p49

45

Cwm Clydach

Cwm Clydach
Clydach

From M4 J45, take B4630 to Clydach village. Go past second turning on left signed to Craig Felin. At mini roundabout turn left and follow through housing area for 1.5km (1 mile). At bottom of hill over small bridge, car park is signed on right. (SN684025) 86 ha (211 acres)

RSPB

The upland oak woodland reserve lining the sides of the Clydach valley has developed since the 1960s, when mining stopped in the area.

Today there are still signs of the industrial past but now the site is populated with oak, birch, ash, alder, sycamore, willow and hazel – all dripping in wet mosses, liverworts and graceful ferns, while swathes of bramble hang over sections of the bank.

The river can be a raging torrent, with the overwhelming noise of rushing water a constant companion. And while there are some great walks on a well-surfaced path, care is needed with children.

In and around the river you can spot dragonflies, fish and birds such as dippers and grey wagtails. Other birds to look out for include redstart, pied flycatcher and buzzard.

Man's influence is seen in the form of planted, non-native species such as buddleia, raspberry and Japanese knotweed which line the path edge.

Clyne Valley Country Park

Clyne Valley Country Park
Swansea

Follow signs for Mumbles on A4067, turning right by the side of the petrol station. Car park on left. (SS610915) 243 ha (600 acres)

Swansea County Council

Popular with dog walkers, cyclists and grey squirrels alike, this mature oak, ash and beech woodland envelopes part of the Sustrans route 4 cycle track, thanks to an adapted disused railway track.

The path, about 8ft wide, smooth and with a very easy gradient, leads along a raised embankment with a brook on one side and woodland on the other. This is dominated by ash, with alder, birch, sycamore, willow and hazel and the invasive Himalayan balsam growing vigorously by the water.

The noise of nearby roads and houses fades as you get deeper into the wood and the pathway eventually forks, with timber bridges over the brooks and small paths leading deeper into the wood.

Further on there is a large pond, popular with local fishermen, with areas of rhododendron, old hawthorn and fine specimen trees.

MAP 2

Bishops Wood
Caswell

From Swansea follow signs to Mumbles then right at mini roundabout by White Rose pub and follow signs to Caswell. Passing Summer Cliff chalet park on left, car park at bottom of hill on right, opposite beach. (SS594879)
19 ha (46 acres)
Swansea County Council

Bishops Wood

Designated a local nature reserve, this site is a mosaic of limestone, grassland, woodland – some of it ancient – and scrub crossed by nature trails varying from half to one-and-a-quarter miles.

Set right by the beach, it is a lovely place to walk and is particularly suitable for children and people with disabilities, though some challenging walks can be had up the valley sides.

Circular paths lead to the cliff top, with sea views and in summer, expect to be accompanied by either a brimstone, orange-tip or speckled wood butterfly.

The valley sides are cloaked in a canopy of oak and ash above a shrub layer of hazel and holly. And beneath the shrubs look for herb Paris, early purple orchid, dog's violet, dog's mercury and wild garlic.

A cottage on the site was once the summer retreat of John Dilwyn Llewelyn of Penllegaer.

Bishopston Valley
Bishopston

On B4436 take turning into Church Lane (look for Winston Hotel sign) to Bishopston. Park opposite St Teilo's Church and walk down to ford where entrance to site can be see on other side of ford and to left. (SS575894)
49 ha (120 acres) SSSI

National Trust

Bishopston is strictly for the fit. The riverbed of the steep-sided limestone valley forms the footpath through the top third. While this is largely dry in summer, the path can flood so boots are recommended.

The path follows beside a quarried 'gorge' flanked with dramatic 50ft-high sheer cliff faces. The bottom is covered in the large round leaves of butterbur while the sides are festooned with ivy and old man's beard, lending a 'Jurassic Park' air to the site. These pits, which flood with water after heavy rain, are a distinctive feature.

Oak, ash and elm populate the ancient woodland in the bottom half of the valley together with small-leaved lime and wild service trees. Deadwood litters the valley floor, providing excellent habitats for invertebrates and adding to the jungle atmosphere. Visitors in spring can enjoy impressive carpets of wild garlic.

As the river runs to the sea it flows through wet meadows at Widegate and reedbeds at Pwll Du to emerge through a shingle bank into Pwll Du Bay.

Bishopston Valley

MAP 2

Park Wood
Park Mill

Turn off A4118 into the Gower Heritage Centre. Follow signs for Parc le Breos and use car park surrounded by cleft oak railings (SS543892) 100 ha (247 acres)

Forestry Commission

Majestic trees emerge from the damp, sheltered and fertile soils of this gently sloping wooded valley. And thanks to some excellent wide forest drives, the whole family can enjoy easy access to the mixed woodland, with its veteran oaks, beech and fine ash woods of European importance.

Buzzards, woodpeckers and nuthatch are resident, along with both lesser and greater horseshoe bats.

The valley floor is wide and level, with mown grass giving the impression of a grand entrance to an estate. Look out for the impressive burial chamber of Parc le Breos, dating back to between 3000 and 1,900BC. The trees on the woodland edges here – both broadleaf and conifer – are magnificent.

Broadleaves dominate the site and there are some fine veteran oaks on the southern side where the ground is higher and drier. Vegetation is vigorous, with willow herb, brambles and meadow sweet at your feet.

Park Wood

Gelli Hir Wood

Gelli Hir Wood
Three Crosses

Fork right off A4118 at Upper Killay. Then take second right off Fairwood Common. Wood is on right with layby on left. (SS562925)
11ha (27 acres)
Wildlife Trust of South and West Wales

The next time you're travelling the main route through Gower, heading for the beaches, take some time to pop into this dense, lush woodland just off Fairwood Common.

A beautifully carved name sign welcomes you to this relatively level site, where lucky visitors may glimpse silver-washed fritillary butterflies along the sunny rides or even a shy dormouse.

Alongside the wide main ride are old wood banks and occasional mature oaks, along with some small-leaved lime trees which are of particular interest.

Scored with numerous streams and ditches, the damp, dense woodland is full of ash, birch, alder and oak with lots of natural regeneration and an understorey of hazel, hawthorn, holly and dog rose. Moss, liverworts and ferns abound. Here and there on drier ground are heather, scabious and tormentil, and bluebells make a fine show in the south.

Hidden deeper inside is a large pond, covered in reed mace and burweed, which boasts a bird hide.

MAP 2

Oxwich Woods

Oxwich &
Nicolaston Woods
Oxwich

Go past shops on the left in
Oxwich, following signs for Oxwich
castle. Layby and site entrance on
left. (SS498883) 10 ha (25 acres)
AONB SSSI

Countryside Council for Wales

Oxwich and Nicolaston Woods
line steep slopes that form
'bookends' to Oxwich Bay, one
of the most diverse coastal
habits in the UK.

This national nature reserve
features sand dunes, rocky
shores, meadows, marshes, open
water, streams, reedbeds and
heathland too, all within a few
miles of the coastline.

The site's almost landscaped
finish is complemented by some
tremendous conifers, gnarled
and twisted by the sea winds.

A narrow pathway runs
through Oxwich woods, up
gently ascending slopes. At the
bottom are large sycamores and
oaks and nearer the top much
smaller trees, with gorse and
hazel giving way to bracken at
the very top of the wood,
where Oxwich Castle is sited.

Other paths drop away down
hundreds of tiny steps to a
precipitous cliff edge with
views across the bay to
Nicolaston Wood. This example
of semi-natural oak woods –
with mature conifers adding
diversity – is beautifully set
above the sand dunes.

Mill Wood
Oxwich

Follow A4118 and turn left after
passing both Nicolaston and
parkland of the Penrice estate.
(SS492882) 110 ha (272 acres)
AONB
Forestry Commission

Mill Wood

Towering alder, ash and oak
trees and a purpose-made
wheelchair-accessible kissing
gate greet the visitor to this
peaceful woodland, just one
mile from Oxwich beach.

Easy-going forest tracks soon
lead you past the repaired ruins
of a former watermill, once
part of the Penrice estate. Look
out for the stone grinding
wheels and you can trace the
route of the water from the
leat to where the wheel once
rotated.

Further on is a lovely large
pond that supplied water for
the mill, where remnants of the
leat are still evident. A bench
near the water's edge provides
a good vantage point for
watching moorhens dabble
about among the pond weed
and tall reed mace. Otters have
been spotted here.

Because the woodland is
sheltered from strong winds, it
is damp and fertile and the
vegetation includes willow
herb, large equisetum and
meadowsweet, along with
introduced species such as
rhododendron.

MAP 2

Cwym Ivy Woods
Llanmadoc

At the tip of Gower. Park in Llanmadoc and turn right, opposite church. Walk down, past pink house on right to timber gate with walking signpost. Path starts here. (SS442937) 11 ha (26 acres) SSSI

Wildlife Trust of South and West Wales

Mainly ancient woodland, Cwym Ivy Woods cover two sites nestling close to the scenic Burry inlet.

The first narrow strip hugs steep slopes, with delightful views across to the pines, dunes and sea at Whiteford sands, at times hidden by blackthorn, elder, columbine and clematis.

The path, narrow and often tricky underfoot, dips into woodland dominated by ash, and festooned with old man's beard plus the occasional mature larch and cherry.

While much of the wood is a delight, your gaze will frequently be seaward because the route affords coastal views.

In contrast, the pine belt planted on the dunes of Whiteford Sands is great for families and has a desert island feel. Children can play in the sand amid mature pines on the peninsula, with beautiful views over the Loughor Estuary to Pembrey Country Park.

Cwym Ivy Woods

Pembrey Country Park

Pembrey Country Park
Pembrey

From Carmarthen take A484
signposted Llanelli. At Pembrey
turn right signposted Pembrey
Country Park. (SN396011)
900 ha (2224 acres) SSSI
**Forestry Commission and
Carmarthenshire County Council**

Bunkers, engine sheds and
railway platforms – not the
sights that normally greet a
woodland visitor. But they are
one of the reasons this forest is
here. More than 70 years ago,
Corsican pines were planted to
conceal a Royal Ordnance
factory.

The site is easy to walk and
cycle, thanks to a good
network of level tracks and
paths that wind through the
pine forest that was planted
over an extensive area of
sand dunes.

The woodland is open and
the dunes provide some great
picnic spots – Cefn Sidan's
sandy beach is but a stone's
throw away. Pembrey draws
large numbers of visitors but it
is big enough to allow hours of
walking without seeing
another soul.

Beneath the trees you may
come across small wetland
pockets or dry, grassy banks,
with marram grass, vetches, rest
harrow and southern marsh
orchid. There are ants' nests
and a variety of butterflies
including orange tip and
meadow brown. A bird hide
and lake add interest. Pony
trekking and cycle hire are also
on offer.

MAP 2

Court Wood
Pembrey

When entering Pembrey from the Carmarthen direction turn left besides the Butchers Arms and then right by a grassy triangle up a road 'unsuitable for long vehicles'. Court wood is on the right.
(SN424022) 40 ha (99 acres)
Carmarthenshire County Council

A mixture of oak woodland, green lanes and conifer plantation, this site cloaks a hill rising out of the level land beside Carmarthen Bay and Pembrey Country Park.

The views from the top of the site are well worth the climb, offering vistas across Pembrey, the bay and Gower Peninsula.

However, negotiating a route through the woods requires a large scale OS map and the ascent to the top of the hill is quite a struggle. But this is offset by the tremendous variation in habitats and stunning views. No wonder the spot was used by Iron Age communities as the site for a fortress.

Court Wood is dominated by oaks with a hazel, hawthorn, blackthorn and holly understorey, interspersed with steep but well-maintained paths. Part of the public rights of way crossing the site include the long distance path known as the Ilityd Way, which links Pembrey to Margam Park.

Mynydd Mawr Woodland Park

Tumble

From Crosshands follow B4317 to Tumble. On leaving the village turn right, following brown tourist sign. A tall miner's lamp marks the entrance. (SN538128)
100 ha (250 acres)
Carmarthenshire County Council

Created on land reclaimed from a coalmine in 1979, this thriving and diverse mix of habitats shows how wasteland can be transformed in just a few short years.

The land has been developed as a country park and the unusual mix of soil types means that several habitats appear within a small area. Complemented with some very easy access, it is a great place for families and the less-able visitor.

Habitats include Corsican pine woods, where goldcrests can be spotted, and scrubland of goat willow, ash and silver birch, frequented by bullfinch and long tailed tits.

By the Gwendereath river is a peaceful semi-natural woodland with old oaks, hazel, marsh marigold and the nationally rare whorled caraway

There is also wetland with alder, goat willow and purple loosestrife, and all can be explored thanks to a level and well-surfaced circular walk, with more challenging paths leading deeper into the woodland.

Mynydd Mawr Woodland Park

MAP 2

Carmel
Gorslas
Take A476 from Crosshands. After
3km (2 miles) there is a small right
turn to Llandybie. The woodland is
on hill to left. 1.5km (1mile) down
lane, before village of Pentre
Gwenlais, entrance on left.
(SN603165) 30 ha (74 acres) SSSI
**Various including Countryside
Council for Wales**

Carmel

More than 1,000 toads migrate
to the turlough – a pond with
a difference – at the heart of
this woodland each spring. It's
quite a sight.

The oak and ash woodland,
grassland and bogs that make
up Carmel National Nature
Reserve are teeming with life.
They are home to large
butterfly populations, sundews
and mosses, dragonflies, bats,
badgers and dormice, not to
mention bluebells, ransoms and
dog's mercury.

The woodland grows on
limestone outcrops – unusual
here – hence part of the hill
has been quarried. Visitors are
therefore advised to stick to
pathways and keep a keen eye
on children.

At the bottom is a picnic area
where the impressive disused
quarry with its sheer limestone
cliff faces can be seen at their
best. The entrance is framed by
silver birch, goat willow and
wild clematis cascading over
the rock face.

The turlough has no feeder
streams but rises and descends
depending on the level of the
ground water.

Dinefwr Woods
Llandeilo

Follow signs from Llandeilo town
or from the A40 Llandeilo bypass.
(SN625225) 25 ha (62 acres) SSSI
**Wildlife Trust of South and West
Wales and National Trust**

Regarded as probably the best
collection of veteran trees in
Wales and second only to the
royal parks in the UK, this is a
site worth visiting.

Best approached from the
National Trust office in
Newton House, the parkland,
with its majestic oak, horse
chestnut, ash, beech and lime is
grazed by white park cattle and
herds of fallow deer.

At the top of the very steep
slopes stand the ruins of
historic Dinefwr Castle. This is
surrounded by ancient woods,
made up of oak, ash and
sycamore with an understorey
of hazel, bramble, elderberry
and the occasional crab apple.
Its position means this part of
the site is accessible only to the
fit visitor.

Looking out from the castle
you can enjoy some
phenomenal views across the
wide Tywi Valley.

A network of well-used
gravel and earth paths cross the
site and some sections are
suitable for wheelchairs.

Dinefwr Castle

59

MAP 2

Green Castle Woods
Carmarthen/Llangain
Take Llansteffan road from
Carmarthen. Passing some
secondary schools and a leisure
centre, continue along B4321 for a
few miles. After sharp right-hand
bend, car park is 200m on right.
(SN391167)
51 ha (125 acres)
Woodland Trust

This ideal family-friendly
woodland is one of only a few
countryside areas near
Carmarthen with open public
access. No wonder it's popular.

The site is actually made up
of three separate semi-natural
ancient woods, separated by
meadows and bisected by the
Carmarthen to Llansteffen
road. While two are mainly
oak, the third is a varied mix
of birch, ash, alder and willow.

The woodland runs down to
the banks of the tidal Afon
Tywi, which makes a pleasant
diversion for the careful visitor.

There are lots of easier paths
to explore and boardwalks
which allow access to wetter
areas. Some of the meadow
areas were planted with native
species in the mid-1990s and
these are forming a significant

Oak leaves

link between the established ancient woodland sections.

About 14 hectares of grassland remain and the patchwork of small-hedged fields creates a very attractive landscape with views over the Afon Tywi and towards Carmarthen. The Carmarthenshire Coast long distance footpath passes through the site.

St Martin's Wood
Laugharne

Entering Laugharne, past church gate, take left turn up cobbled lane/bridleway and turn right at top. Wood is on left. (SN304115) 7 ha (17 acres)

Woodland Trust

Planted to mark the Millennium, St Martin's Wood is still in its formative years.

There's an unusual look to some of the ash, oak, willow, sweet chestnut and rowan because the prevailing wind has coaxed them into an angle.

Though still maturing, the site still has plenty to interest, with mature trees bordering the site and ancient hedgerows packed with wildlife. Nearby St Martin's churchyard boasts some fine old yews and the grave of Dylan Thomas.

Around the field edges, an unplanted ride provides a popular riding route for local people. If you head for the top you can enjoy views out to sea and back over the town.

A long distance footpath runs along the top edge of the site, along the route of the river Taf toward the Towy Estuary and Green Castle woods near Carmarthen.

There is no on-site parking so it's best to park in historic Laugharne and walk along the cobbled lane that leads up to the wood.

MAP 2

Colby Woodland Gardens
Llanteg

Heading west on A477 turn left
just outside Llanteg. Follow
National Trust signs for Colby.
(SN155081) 20 ha (49 acres)
National Trust

A riot of bluebells, daffodils,
rhododendron and azaleas
transform this woodland
estate into a blaze of colour
in spring.

Its mix of native and exotic
species has evolved since the
early 19th century when the
estate was built by mine-owner
John Colby and later
developed by the Katy family.

Colby House itself is not
open to the public but
provides a picturesque focal
point for the wide, landscaped
valley parkland.

Flanking this are gently
sloping native oak, ash and
sycamore woods, interplanted
with Scots pine, beech,
cypress, copper beech and
Douglas fir and served by
waymarked routes.

Set above the parkland are
ancient coppiced oak woods
called Craig y Borion, which
are home to 45 species of
breeding birds.

Oak dominates, with ash,
birch, holly and some planted
pine, cypress and larch, and all
can be explored via an easy-
going path forming a
horseshoe up and down
the valley.

Colby Woodland Gardens

Stackpole Estate

Stackpole Estate
Stackpole

From Pembroke take the B4319
signed Stackpole. Following signs to
Stackpole you will pass through
the woodland on the way to the
village. (SR982965)
485 ha (1,200 acres) AONB, SSSI
National Trust

A combination of nature and
man's ingenuity has created a
beautiful landscape that
supports a wealth of wildlife of
European importance.

The Stackpole Estate is a
fabulous mix of ancient and
landscaped woodland, lakes,
cliffs and beaches plus Bronze
and Iron Age remains.

Making their homes here are
20 species of dragonfly, 11
species of bat, a dozen or so
wintering duck species,
kingfishers, warblers, water rail
and bunting, tits, treecreeper,
nuthatch and woodpeckers –
not to mention otters.

The owners, the Campbells of
Cawdor, have aided accessibility
to the valley's steep side by
providing stone bridges and
causeways.

Extensive footpaths provide
wheelchair access and mountain
bikes and horse riders are
welcome in parts.

Ash dominates but each
woodland has its own character,
from Lodge Park, once formal
and now reverting to secondary
woodland of sycamore and ash,
to Caroline Grove – a wet
woodland favoured by otters –
and the broadleaf-conifer mix
of Cheriton Bottom and
Castle Dock.

MAP 2

Lawrenny Woods
Lawrenny

Heading north on A4075 from Carew, turn left for Cresswell Quay then follow signs through lanes to Lawrenny. (SN015062) 40 ha (99 acres)

National Trust

Lawrenny sits on the Daucleddau estuary, a river valley flooded by the sea centuries ago, when the ice sheets melted.

The first section seems uninspiring – mainly sycamore with some ash and a woodland floor of brambles. As the land begins to rise you enter a striking semi-natural oak woodland with a rich understorey of hazel, holly, hawthorn, hart's-tongue fern, club rush and honeysuckle, the sounds and smells of the sea in the air.

Occasionally you reach the water's edge to stand on lichen-covered rocks and watch teal, shelduck, wigeon and waders in the estuary. From here, Lawrenny Woods look like a

Lawrenny Woods

neatly trimmed green hedge hugging the coast, such is the effect of the prevailing salty westerlies.

Paths slope gently but are prone to be uneven, narrow and slippery so this walk is for fitter

visitors. It also forms a section of the Landsker Boarderlands Trail, part of a long-distance path around South Pembrokeshire and West Carmarthenshire.

Parking and other facilities provided at the quay.

Little Milford Wood
Haverfordwest
On ring road to south of Haverfordwest take minor road to Llangwm. After 1.5km (1 mile) take left turn signposted Little Milford just outside village of Lower Freystrop. Car park 800m on right. (SM965112) 20 ha (50 acres)
National Trust

If you like your woodland peaceful, visit this quiet mixed site by the muddy estuary shoreline.

Native broadleaves line the gentle valley slopes and wetter areas around two small streams, with conifers growing on more level parts of the site.

Enveloped by beeches, the car park soon leads out to a

recently cleared area where young birch, ash and oak are already beginning to regenerate.

The circular route leads, via a wide track, through a bright and sunny clearing with foxgloves and willow herb, to well-thinned blocks of hemlock.

Numerous mature beech and oak trees add to the interest of the site, growing alongside old stone walls. The bottom of the valley is lined with oak, ash, birch and alder. Flowers like figwort, enchanter's nightshade, wood sorrel and buttercup inhabit the shady and boggy sides of the stream.

Paths radiate out into the Western Cleddu where you can hear oyster catchers and curlews along the shoreline.

MAP 2

Minwear

Minwear
Narberth

Follow A40 westwards past
Narberth. Take right turn to
Blackpool Mill on A4075. A little
way up here turn right. Minwear
layby on right (SN055136)
200 ha (494 acres)
Forestry Commission

This is a small and relatively
young plantation dominated by
beech, with large-leaved red
oak and larch cladding the
gentle slops on the edge of the
Eastern Cleddau.

Little grows beneath the
dense beech canopy but
periodic thinning could see
this change in the future.

Reddish sandstone paths,
occasionally crossed by muddy
streams, make for easy walking
but the site is unsuitable for
wheelchairs, since there are
steps to negotiate.

Running parallel with the
Cleddau along the bottom of
the site is part of the Landsker
Borderlands Trail. A sign leads
from here to a viewing area
overlooking the Eastern
Cleddau and amid the wooded

landscape opposite you can spot the grand Picton Castle.

A block of plantation has been clear-felled, making way for the regeneration of birch trees and millions of seedlings are shooting up amid the heather and bilberry, with one or two very large firs kept for landscape value.

Canaston Wood
Narberth

Follow A40 west of Narberth. Turn left at Canaston bridge onto A4075, entrance to wood on left 800m (0.5 mile) (SN075140) 4850 ha (12,000 acres)
Forestry Commission

There are miles of gravel forest tracks to explore on foot, horseback or bicycle, through this massive ancient woodland site.

There is a lot to discover too. The forest is packed with historic interest and lies in an area rich in ruins associated with the Knights of St John of Jerusalem. There are many Iron Age sites in an around the woods.

Much of the original ancient woodland was felled in the 1950s to make way for Japanese larch, Douglas fir, Norway spruce and some beech. But some mature oaks and beech survive alongside the rides, where birch and goat willow are a common sight. The wood is quite open in parts and teeming with insects.

The presence of the uncommon hay-scented bucker fern confirms the area's long continuity of woodland cover.

The yellow flowering St John's wort, associated with the Crusades, grows alongside willow herb, hogweed, foxglove, wood anemones and bluebells, and nuthatches can also be seen.

MAP 2

Withy Bush Woods
Haverfordwest

Take A40 from Haverfordwest to
Withy Bush. At first roundabout
take road to industrial estate. About
1.5km (1 mile) along car park on
right. (SM962188) 20 ha (49 acres)
Pembrokeshire County Council

Noise from the nearby
industrial estate occasionally
punctuates the peace of this
semi-landscaped woodland,
once part of the 16th century
Withy Bush estate.

During the Second World War,
the house – now demolished –
was a base for RAF pilots who
flew from the nearby
aerodrome. Moss-covered
remnants of the estate buildings
are a reminder of the past.

This level woodland boasts
some tremendous specimen
trees – among them sessile oak,
lime, beech, horse chestnut,
wych elm, ash and sycamore.

In springtime there are
celandine, speedwells, early
purple orchids, primroses,
wood anemones and fern, as
well as redcurrant, a legacy of
the estate days. There is also an
understorey of hazel, cherry
laurel, hawthorn and holly.

Access is aided by a wide
Tarmac path, ideal for
wheelchairs, while a taping rail
around the circular route is
provided for the visually
impaired. Benches are also
provided along the way.

Orchids

Coed Cilgelynnen
Fishguard

From Fishguard follow B4313 for 3km (2 miles) and turn right. Wood is on right. Approaching entrance you can enter via timber gates and park on grassy area beyond but be sure to close gates behind you. (SM979347)
15 ha (36 acres) SSSI
Woodland Trust

Lying on the steep valley sides just two miles from Fishguard lies a peaceful mixed broadleaved woodland of coppiced oak, sycamore, ash, birch, hazel and holly.

On the boggy, sheltered valley floor alder and willow grow alongside Britain's most southwesterly raised bog. Esgyrn Bottom actually supports several bogland plants including bog asphodel, cotton grass and purple moor grass.

A tributary of the River Gwaun passes through the valley, where the trees are home to mosses and beard-like lichen that thrives in the humid conditions and clean air.

Although there is no circular route through the wood, exploration along the track and grassy path is a peaceful experience and the return route is certain to spring new discoveries on the visitor.

Hazelnuts

MAP 2

The Gwaun Valley
Fishguard

Take B4313 from Fishguard. After Llanychaer take next left down narrow minor lane. Car parks and several footpaths lead into woods off this lane. Parking at Cilrhedyn Bridge, Pontfaen and Sychpant.
(SN025341) 200 ha (494 acres)

Various including Pembrokeshire Coast National Park

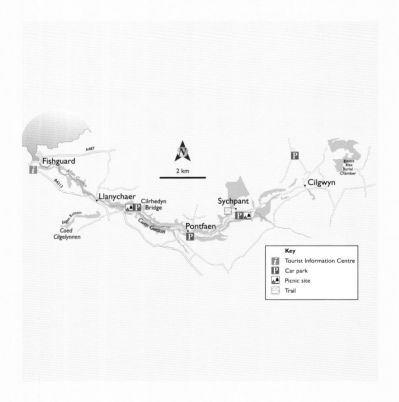

The Gwaun Valley

A hugely important site, the Gwaun Valley – cloaked in broadleaved woods – is one of few places where high quality, semi-natural ancient woodland stretches from river source to mouth. As such, it is a wildlife treasure trove

The woodland is dominated by oak with occasional birch, sycamore, ash and planted beech and conifers, although work is underway to return the whole valley to broadleaved woods in future years.

The valley was widened and re-landscaped by glaciers during the Ice Age, resulting in some fertile river meadows and valley side paths with fine views through the woodlands. The Gwaun snakes its way through this roomy valley floor which provides a home for otters that hide among the alder roots.

Towards the top of the river the waterlogged valley, uneconomical to farm, has evolved into a wilderness of birch, willow and alder. In autumn the colours here are stunning and in spring the bluebells and anemones well worth the trip.

MAP 1

Paths range from wide tracks to narrow, steep pathways and some circular routes but an Ordnance Survey map is recommended. Just off the path from Cilrhedyn Bridge entrance is a small tunnel (an old mine adit) that adds mystery and atmosphere to the woodland walk.

Conifers have been felled in places, providing excellent views over to the deciduous valley sides opposite.

Welsh black cattle graze the fertile meadows, and the visitor should look out for the white-and-liver coats and long sweeping horns of the rare British longhorn herd that grazes the valley sides.

Right at the top of the valley is a car park for the Pentre Ifan burial chamber, the largest Portal Dolmen in Wales, built 3,500 years BC. From here you can enjoy a walk to Tycanol and Pentre Ifan woods. Both ancient woodland, Pentre Ifan was partially planted with conifers in the 1960s. Here, again, the conifers have mostly been felled to make way for native oak woodland.

The Gwaun Valley

Pengelli Forest
Eglwyswrw

Turn off A487 in Felindre Fachog
along narrow road and over ford.
1.5km (1 mile) further on, layby on
left and woodland on right. Or
from Eglwyswrw, take minor road
north for about 1.5km (1 mile).
(SN130393) 65 ha (160 acres)
**Wildlife Trust of South and
West Wales**

Regarded by some as the
country's most beautiful
woodland, Pengelli forms part
of the largest ancient
woodland in Wales.

Oaks, felled to make charcoal
for the leather industry,
opened up sunny glades where
insects such as purple
hairstreak and silver-washed
fritillary butterflies thrive.

The wood is managed to
encourage a diversity of wildlife
which ranges from dormouse to
golden-ringed dragonflies and
dark bush crickets. The rare
barbastelle is one of eight bat
species found here. Cow-wheat,
bluebells and wood anemones
grow alongside adder's-tongue
fern, bastard balm, violets
and sanicle.

There are two distinct areas
to this wood. Oaks
interspersed with rowan, birch
and holly have a sparse
understorey of bilberry,
heather and honeysuckle in
areas that were cleared of trees
early last century. Where the
understorey is dense indicates
areas which have never been
clear-felled.

An excellent network of
paths serves four waymarked
routes and your walk will be
rewarded with some lovely
views of the Preseli Hills.

MAP 2

Brechfa Forest
Brechfa/Abergorlech

From Carmarthen take A40. In Nantgaredig turn left onto B4310, signposted Brechfa. (SN571353)
5000 ha (12,350 acres)
Forestry Commission

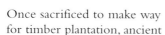

Once sacrificed to make way for timber plantation, ancient woodland species are making a welcome comeback across this vast site.

Conifers are being thinned and removed to encourage bluebells, cowslips, ferns and dog's mercury and to allow veteran broadleaves to thrive again.

The site is still dominated by conifers but occasionally hardwood crops such as beech exist amid the miles of forest tracks and footpaths that draw walkers, riders and cyclists.

The area has a wealth of archaeological features, with Iron Age forts, standing stones and field boundaries.

There are several entrances, the two main points being at Brygwm and Abergorlech. At the first, visitors walk beneath towering Douglas firs more than 60 years old. At Abergorlech the woodland is a broadleaf-conifer mix at the start of an ambitious new mountain bike route alongside the fast-flowing Gorlech.

The site is well used by birds of prey – look out for peregrines, red kites, buzzards and hawks.

Brechfa Forest

Talley Woods
Talley

Talley can be reached from Brechfa Forest or by taking B4302 from just outside Llandeilo. Turn left in the village of Talley, signposted The Abbey. Woodland is on the steep slopes over looking the village. (SN628324) 85 ha (210 acres)
Forestry Commission

A newly-built gravel track forms the two-and-a-half mile backbone of a circular route around the woods which line the steep slopes overlooking the village of Talley.

The walk, steep in parts, is well worth the effort to drink in the views from the top of the village to the impressive ruins of 12th century Talley Abbey and two lakes. The village also boasts a pretty church and several other estate houses around the abbey ruins.

There are two woodland blocks, mainly coniferous, with some broadleaved trees lining the edges. The site also has an area of newly planted broadleaves.

Efforts by the local councils, development agencies and the community – spearheaded by the Talley Community Amenity Association – have boosted public access to the site, which offers a choice of paths for active walkers to try. Cyclists and horse riders are also welcome on the main track.

Talley Woods framed by Abbey ruins

75

MAP 3

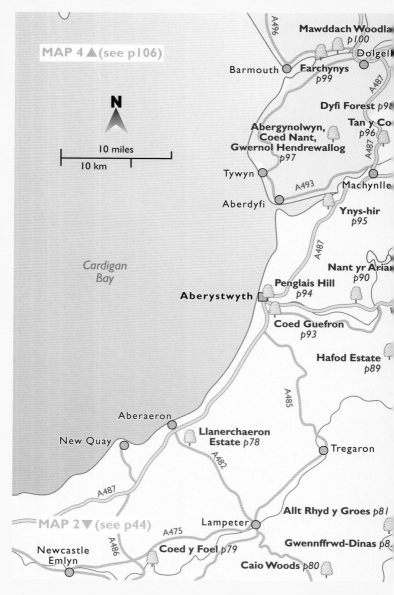

MAP 4 ▲ (see p106)

N

10 miles
10 km

Cardigan
Bay

Mawddach Woodla
p100

Dolgel

Barmouth   Farchynys
p99

Dyfi Forest p9

Abergynolwyn,   Tan y Co
Coed Nant,   p96
Gwernol Hendrewallog
p97

Tywyn

A493

Machynlle

Aberdyfi

Ynys-hir
p95

A487

Nant yr Aria
p90

Penglais Hill
p94

Aberystwyth

Coed Guefron
p93

Hafod Estate
p89

A485

Aberaeron

Llanerchaeron
Estate p78

New Quay

Tregaron

A482

MAP 2 ▼ (see p44)

A475

Lampeter

Allt Rhyd y Groes p81

Newcastle
Emlyn

A486

Coed y Foel p79

Gwennffrwd-Dinas p8

Caio Woods p80

76

Lake Vyrnwy *p102*

470

A458

Mallwyd

A458

Breidden *p105*

A483

Gaer Fawr Wood *p101*

A458

Welshpool

A458

Montgomery

A470

A483

A489

A488

Coed Gwernafon *p88*

Newtown

Bishop's Castle

Llanidloes

A470

Cefn Cenarth *p87*

Llangurig

A470

Rhayader

Knighton

A488

Elan Valley *p86*

Llandrindod Wells

Presteigne
Silia Wood *p85*

A44

Bailey Einon *p86*

Kington

Irfon *p84*

A483

Builth Wells

A481

MAP 1 ▼ (see p18)

A470

Cwm Byddog *p84*

A438

Halfway and Crychan *p83*

A470

A438

Hay-on-Wye

77

MAP 3

Llanerchaeron estate
Aberaeron

Take A482 from Aberaeron.
In 3 km (2 miles) take road to left
signed Llanerchaeron (SN480605)
50 ha (124 acres)
National Trust

The Llanerchaeron estate, a rare
example of a self-sufficient
agricultural estate, boasts walled
kitchen gardens, orchards, farm
buildings and a restored house
redesigned in the 18th century
by John Nash.

The woods that line the steep
river-valley sides of the wider
estate can be explored for free
and there are several walks that
take the visitor through flower-
rich meadows, farmland,
riverside and the rich semi-
natural broadleaved woodland.

Ash, oak, sycamore, birch,
alder and willow can all be
found, along with some mature
exotic trees, among them
conifers, beech, copper beech
and sweet chestnut planted in
the picturesque landscaping
style of Humphrey Repton.

The woodland paths lead past
veteran and mature ash and
oak, with bluebells, wood
anemones and primroses
coming to life in spring and
campion in summer.

You can enjoy superb views
along the valley to the house
and the town of Aberaeron.

Coed y Foel
Llandysul

Take B4476, signed Pren-gwyn from Llandysul for 1.5km (1 mile), turn first right next to detached house, continue for 800m (0.5 mile) to car park on left. (SN428425)
24 ha (58 acres)
Woodland Trust

A local landmark, easily spotted from nearby Llandysul, Coed y Foel clothes the south-facing slopes of the Gwenffrwdd valley.

It is a semi-natural ancient woodland of sessile oak where, in spring, the lower section becomes a mass of bluebells and wood anemones. Bilberries, ferns, mosses and grasses are widespread throughout, along with a holly understorey.

Leading from the ample car park is an easy, wide, stone-surfaced ride to the stream, which is crossed by a culvert and footbridge. From here the walk takes in a steep track before reaching level walking along the bottom of the wood, a good place to enjoy the views across sheep-grazed pasture on the opposite valley side.

At the end of the wood a path doubles back to form a circular walk that takes you up to 200m above sea level at the top of the site. The higher you climb, the more sparse the woodland, and the views open up.

Bluebells adding their spring colour

Caio Woods

Caio Woods
Caio

Take A482 north, turning right just before Pumsaint, home of the Dolaucothi National Trust Goldmines. The village of Caio is at the southern end of Caio woods. (SN679405) 1000ha (2470 acres)
Forestry Commission

In contrast with the more open, rugged woodlands of mid-upland Wales, this mixed conifer forest has a cosy feel, hemmed in by dense conifers and patches of bilberry.

The site overlooks the fertile farming area of the Cothi valley, with moorland and forestry plantations to the north and small dairy farms and hamlets south and west.

A choice of entrances offer access to the plantation. The main one offers several waymarked routes through the gently-sloping woodland. The area around the car park, partially wooded with silver birch and wild cherry, is set beside a pretty stream.

Another entrance lies just outside the village, where a gravel forest track alongside the edge of a pungent-smelling pine forest gives views across the rolling countryside. Further on are areas of larch with sunny rides edged with heather, bracken and gorse. Further still, spruce and fir thrive on level land, making this a good route for riders and cyclists.

Allt Rhyd y Groes

Allt Rhyd y Groes
Llandovery

From RSPB Dinas reserve drive
south towards Llandovery, turning
left at first bridge. Pull onto grass
verge before next iron bridge.
(SN769475) 20 ha (49 acres)

Countryside Council for Wales

If you are looking for a
challenge from a woodland visit
– this site fits the bill.

It's quite a walk from the iron
bridge – about 540 yards along
an old green lane to the foot of
the wood. The stone-surfaced
lane is often slippery, so this is a
walk for the relatively fit.

Once inside the woodland
that cloaks the steep slopes, you
are among typical upland sessile
oak with birch, hazel, alder,
goat willow and ash growing
by the streams. The trees are
straighter closer to the shelter
of the valley floor. Occasionally
you encounter older – and
quite awesome – trees.

Sorrel forms dense patches in
sheltered hollows between
rocks and roots, with opposite-
leaved saxifrage and several
nationally rare mosses and
lichens.

The northern section's
beautiful, steep hillside of scree,
boulders and rocky outcrops is
lightly grazed by sheep.

Caution is essential, as much
of the area was once mined and
there are disused mine shafts on
the site.

MAP 3

Gwenffrwd-Dinas
Llandovery

1.5km (1 mile) south of Llyn Brianne dam, just north of Llandovery. (SN788471) SSSI
RSPB

Dinas is an oak woodland draping a steep, rugged hill that separates the fast-flowing river Tywi from the road.

For those able to tackle the slopes, it gives a good idea of

Gwenffrwd-Dinas

what the Welsh uplands looked like at the end of the 13th century. On the sheltered, eastern side are tall, well-grown trees while those on the more exposed northeastern side are gnarled and twisted.

There are some birch and the poorly drained wet areas are home to mosses, liverworts and ferns, which grow among goat willow and alder.

A long, winding boardwalk leads from the car park to the hill. It is not suitable for wheelchairs, otherwise it's great access into a wet wood.

Red kites soar overhead and in summer, golden-ringed dragonflies drift over the mountain streams while pied flycatchers, wood warblers and redstarts breed on the woodland edge. The heather moorland is summer home to wheatears and whinchats.

Halfway & Crychan
Sennybridge
From Llandovery, take A40 Brecon road through wooded valley. Turn left in village of Halfway. Follow signs. (SN848416)
2500ha (6178 acres)
Forestry Commission

You could spend months exploring the hundreds of miles of tracks and paths woven through the thousands of acres of forest that make up Crychan and Halfway – and never leave the wood.

En route you encounter disused quarries, streams and fords, mountain streams, uphill tracks – and magnificent views over the sheep-grazed moors and conifer forests in the Rywi Valley and the Epynt fringes.

Look out for buzzards and red kites soaring above. It is less peaceful when rally driving events are staged here; the forest's hairpin bends and tracks providing thrilling challenges.

The rides and areas of clear-felled conifer are filled with a profusion of heather, ferns, gorse, foxglove and willow herb. Trees of varying size and age add interest and the sweet smell of pine is never far away.

Horse trails and cycle routes interlink with the four car parks and from here it's possible to access the long distance Epynt Way bridleway.

MAP 3

Irfon Forest
Llanwrtyd Wells

Follow signs for Abergwesyn pass
from Llanwrtyd Wells. (SN855508)
1200 ha (2965 acres)
Forestry Commission

A steep hillside broadleaf and
conifer woodland with rocky
outcrops lend the Irfon Forest
an upland feel.

The river runs over huge
limestone boulders worn
smooth and there are also many
standing stones in the area.

The first entrance is at Cwm
Iron where the forest track rises
up through the steep-sided
larch plantation, to a turning

circle from where you can
appreciate the views across the
valley. Fern, willow herb, scrub
oak and birch all thrive in areas
where the larch has been
thinned.

Further along is the main
forest block, called Pwil Bo,
where birch, alder and mature
larch line the stream and picnic
tables provide a great family
stop.

An excellent network of
tracks lead through the conifer
plantation of spruce and
Douglas fir, which can enjoyed
on foot, on horseback, and
mountain bikes.

Another entrance, with a
picnic area, can be found at
Nant y Brain.

Cwm Byddog
Clyro

From Clyro village take unclassified
road north toward Painscastle.
After 800m (0.5 mile) opposite
track to Court Evan Gwynne on
right is gateway to reserve on left.
Park here, avoiding obstruction to
the track. (SO216448)
3 ha (8 acres)
Radnorshire Wildlife Trust

Some of the oldest trees in
Radnorshire are found in this
small but important woodland.

Its massive pollarded oaks
date back up to 450 years –
the largest has a girth of
more than 20ft – and a visit to
the site is worth making for
these alone.

The ancient trees, which
help support more than
100 different species of
epiphytes, including mosses
and lichens, are not the only

links with the past. The remains of a 12th century motte and bailey can be seen close to the entrance. Scrub on this section is an important habitat for birds including yellowhammer, blackcap and garden warbler.

In spring the wood is a carpet of wildflowers, with swathes of bluebells and frequent beds of yellow archangel, cuckoo pint and moschatel. Small mammals on the reserve include the bank vole, yellow-necked mouse and nationally rare dormouse.

Look for alternate-leaved golden saxifrage growing by the stream.

Silia Wood
Presteigne

Take the Evenjob road from Presteigne. Entrance to wood is on right opposite a small group of houses. As there is no parking here, park in Presteigne and walk back to entrance which is along a short section of hedged track connecting the wood with Slough Road. (SO305640) 4 ha (9 acres)
Woodland Trust

Some of the oldest and largest specimen conifers in Wales can be found in the grounds of Silia House.

They include magnificent Douglas fir towering more than 100ft tall and notable specimens of grand fir, noble fir, Wellingtonia and western hemlock. The site is an important skyline feature, easily spotted from the nearby town of Presteigne.

Surrounded by improved grassland, this former ancient woodland lies on a moderately sloping hillside where some of its origins are evident. Bluebell, dog's mercury, yellow archangel and wood sedge grow and much of the canopy is oak and ash. There is also an abundance of non-native shrubs and flowers including flowering currants, box and butcher's broom.

An abundance of non-native shrubs and flowers bring their own characteristics to bear.

There is a circular walk, and a network of paths gives access to all parts of the wood, though they can be steep and narrow.

85

MAP 3

Bailey Einon
Llandrindod Wells

Heading south on A483 in the centre of Llandrindod Wells turn left down Cefnllys Lane. After 2km (1.5 miles) reserve entrance is marked by kissing-gate adjacent to Shaky Bridge. Park at picnic site close to river. (SO083613)
4.5 ha (11 acres) SSSI
Radnorshire Wildlife Trust

The rushing sound of the River Ithon is a constant companion on a tour of this delightful woodland, which is rich in life.

This site is an important spot for early purple orchids and is also home to the locally rare orpine and hairy St John's wort and the grass, lesser hairy-brome. Swathes of bluebells cover sections of the wood and there are also dog's mercury, red campion and yellow archangel.

More than 40 breeding species of bird can be found here – including the pied flycatcher, redstart, great and lesser-spotted woodpecker and garden warbler, while sand martin and dipper are common on the river.

The woodland, a mix of alder and ash above hazel, is a combination of high forest and coppice. It is rich in lichens, mosses, liverworts and insects including important beetle communities. Dragonflies and damselflies are commonly seen darting over the river.

Elan Valley Woods
Rhayader

From Rhayader take B4518 signed Elan Valley. Park at visitor information centre and pick up directions to woods.
(SN928646)
400 ha (1,000 acres) SSSI
RSPB, Elan Trust and Welsh Water

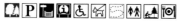

To call the Elan Valley one of Wales' best-kept secrets is an understatement. Around every corner a stunning landscape unfolds. This really is a different world.

Forests and beautiful deciduous woodlands are perched above Elan village, with reservoirs sandwiched between water and moorland. It's a big landscape, and worth spending a couple of days really enjoying the 'outdoor experience' on offer.

There are lots of car parks, an excellent cycle route and paths which help visitors access some 70 miles of hill, valley, reservoirs and woodland.

The broadleaved woodlands, which include the RSPB reserve Carngafallt, are dominated by sessile oak – a wonder to behold and dripping with mosses, liverworts, fungi and ferns.

Birds abound and there is plenty of insect life. In spring, the woodland floor is carpeted with bluebells, primroses, wood anemones, tormentil, wood sorrel and lesser celandine.

The valley also has coniferous plantations, some of which are being gradually replaced with broadleaf trees.

Cefn Cenarth
Rhayader

Take B4518 from Rhayader north to Pant-y-dwr. Follow minor road in centre of village to the west for 1.5km (1 mile). Entrance to Cefn Cenarth south on right with a number of laybys to park in. To reach Cefn Cenarth North walk north along lane and take track directly ahead, when lane takes sharp left. Follow track past the conifer plantation for 400m. Entrance on right through gate. (Cefn Cenarth South SN965757), (Cefn Cenarth North SN967763) 10 ha (24 acres)
Radnorshire Wildlife Trust

Not the easiest site to get to or get around, this woodland is part of a larger complex of woods on the steep hillsides of Cefn Cenarth.

Access from the nearby village is via a very narrow lane and the southern section of the woodland has no designated paths. The northern half has a couple of narrow, marked footpaths leading sure-footed visitors up the hillside.

But for those willing to persevere, these are lovely woods. Sessile oak dominates with rowan while bilberry and cow-wheat occur frequently in the moss-covered ground layer.

Nationally scarce lichens can be found here and the woods are home to 34 different species of breeding birds, among them pied flycatcher, wood warbler, redstart ▶▶

87

MAP 3

and spotted flycatcher, along with three different woodpecker species, tawny owl, coal tit, song thrush and treecreeper.

The green oak tortrix moth is common while the cow-wheat shield bug and brassy-coloured ground beetle can found, along with the oak-feeding longhorn beetle.

Coed Gwernafon
Llanidloes

Follow B4518 west of Llanidloes (signposted Machynlleth via narrow mountain road). Turn right down minor road just after you pass the Bwlch-y-Gle dam and car park on the Llyn Clywedog reservoir, then next left. Drive through the wood and park on right just before second cattle grid. (SN926903) 30 ha (75 acres) SSSI

Woodland Trust

Part of a larger area of ancient woodland designated a Site of Special Scientific Interest (SSSI), this site represents a typical upland oak wood.

Set near the River Trannon west of Llawr y Glyn, the wood is rich in twisted oak coppice, with a fringe of tall, mature oaks at the entrance and furthest end of the site.

Other parts are dense in birch and oak coppice, divided by west-flowing streams that run in deep gullies. Here the occasional ash grows along with plants associated with more damp and fertile woodland flushes.

A path leading through the wood provides a circular walk that runs along the lower edge, running back across steeper sections. Small bridges straddle the steep-sided gullies that carry streams to the river valley below.

Above the wood is pasture but the upper margins of the slope are dominated by bracken and gorse, with some young birch, rowan and oak.

Hafod Estate
Devils Bridge

From Devils Bridge follow B4574 for 3km (2 miles) passing under the arch. Then take the next right sighposted Adas Pwllpeiran and at next junction turn right back onto B4574. Then follow signs to Hafod car park. (SN768737)

250ha (800 acres) SSSI

Forestry Commission and Hafod Trust

Anyone who thought conifer woodlands were all alike should visit this lovingly restored estate, set in the gently sloping, sheltered Yetwyth Valley.

This is an internationally important landscape, designated a Site of Special Scientific Interest (SSSI).

It includes no fewer than four scheduled monuments and several listed buildings within its boundary, along with semi-natural ancient oak woodland noted for its lichens, liverworts, mosses and ferns.

The estate stretches across nearly 800 acres and was planted in the late 18th century by Thomas Jones. His hand is evident at every turn, from the stables and estate houses to the bridges, paths, ice house, monuments, waterfalls and cascade that form an integral part of a beautifully serene location.

There are five routes to explore, all well maintained and offering a unique woodland experience. The scenery varies from open parkland to narrow, wooded valleys and rushing streams, dotted with some of the biggest and oldest specimen trees of their kind in Wales.

MAP 3

Nant yr Arian
Capel Bangor

Take A44 from Aberystwyth signed Capel Bangor. Do not turn off for
Machynlleth but continue through Goginan. Nant yr Arian is on left at top
of long winding hill. (SN718813) 900 ha (2224 acres)
Forestry Commission

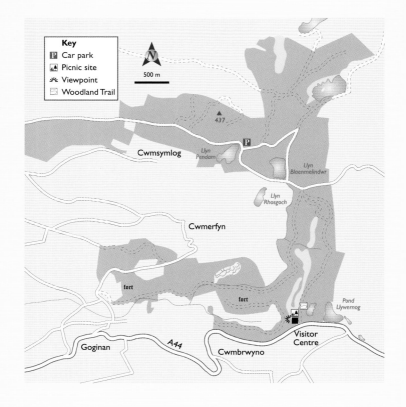

Key
P Car park
Picnic site
Viewpoint
Woodland Trail

500 m

437

Cwmsymlog

Llyn Pendam

Llyn Blaenmelindwr

Llyn Rhosgoch

Cwmerfyn

fort

fort

Pond Llywernog

Visitor Centre

Goginan

A44

Cwmbrwyno

Nant yr Arian

Birds galore, breathtaking views, leisure challenges and a newly opened flagship visitor centre all add to the blend and make this site well worth a visit.

Nant yr Arian lies in the heavily wooded Rhiedol valley, one of the two principal valleys draining water off the mid-Wales hills into Cardigan Bay. Extensively wooded, it has lots of attractions to keep the visitor intrigued.

There are excellent facilities, from play areas and a café with lakeside views, to challenging mountain bike trails and a superb hide allowing some spectacular bird watching.

The area has historically been extensively mined for minerals, leaving behind a legacy of interesting industrial archaeology. The site is also the focus for regular folklore and heritage displays.

And then there are the wonderful views over the Melindwr Valley down to Cardigan Bay where you can see blocks of conifer woodland being transformed to broadleaves as part of a long-term plan by the Forestry Commission to return the

MAP 3

valley to its natural state.

There is a lake, set against the backdrop of towering pines and larch, where felling has allowed heather, gorse and birch to flourish.

Red kites and buzzards circle spectacularly overhead and the RSPB are often on hand to give help and advice about winged residents including raven, nuthatch, robin, tits, whinchat, mallard and pied wagtail. There is also a bird hide where you can enjoy the spectacle of the kites being fed – along with some impressive aerial acrobatics.

A circular walk around the lake offers easy exploration and it is well-surfaced, giving access to all. The route is lined with benches and timber sculptures, along with novel information panels for the children.

There is also a variety of waymarked routes, ranging from a two-thirds-of –a-mile all-abilities walk to a three-mile trek along the ridge top.

Nant yr Arian

Coed Geufron
Aberystwyth

You can cycle or walk from
Aberystwyth to this wood. A path
leading from the prom will take
you to the site then on to Coed y
Bobol and Devil's Bridge. Park in
town. You can also park in the
industrial estate off the Llangurig
road and enter from that side.
(SN601801) 10 ha (24 acres) SSSI
Woodland Trust

Planted in conjunction with
the local community in
Millennium year with oak,
ash, alder, and willow, Coed
Geufron lies in the fertile
valley of the Afon Rheidol as
it meanders its way across this
wide glacial valley to the sea.

  Some parts of the site are
wet, with an interesting and
quite uncommon woodland
habitat featuring goat willow,
alder and downy birch, which
supports a variety of insects
and birds. Other sections are
dry, thanks to the easy-
draining gravel soil, while
gorse- and blackthorn-covered
areas are home to insects
and birds.

  One area is regularly mown
as a hay meadow and makes a
good place to enjoy a picnic.

  Follow the tarmac cycle
route up through the oak
woodland lining the valley
sides, to Devil's bridge, home
of famous waterfalls and steep
oak woods. Further on is
Coed y Bobol, another
recently planted community
woodland where conifers have
been replaced with native
trees for local residents
to enjoy.

MAP 3

Penglais Hill
Aberystwyth

Climbing out of Aberystwyth on the A487 look for small turning on left, beside white lodge, which has stone pillars either side. This is opposite the university. Walk down footpath on left by street lamp. (SN588821) 10 ha (25 acres)

University of Aberystwyth and Ceredigion County Council

Visit Aberystwyth and you're never far from this broadleaved woodland, which forms its northern backdrop.

Visible from anywhere in town, its entrance is a little less obvious – just a small footpath disc that points away from the large glass houses of the university, which owns part of the site.

Once inside there is access to an information panel and a good network of footpaths that take you around the woodland, a mix of oak, huge beech trees, larch, laurel, rhododendron, holly, cherry, elderberry, oak and ash, with more recent self-set sycamore.

A circular walk leads behind a large Victorian house, of whose landscaped grounds the woods probably once formed part. Occasionally large beech trees grow in open areas with little growing in the shade of their leaves. Generations of students appear to have carved their names in the trunks – see if you can spot that of Prince Charles, who studied here for a while.

Penglais Hill

Ynys-hir
Furnace

As you leave the village of Furnace on A487 north of Aberystwyth follow brown tourist signs for Ynys-hir to left. (SN680961)
600 ha (1483 acres) SSSI
RSPB

Visit this beautiful landscape at any time and you will be treated to a superb variety of birds.

Some can be observed from a picnic area close to the visitor centre and overlooking the lake.

Set on a beautiful stretch of lowland, the mixed broadleaf woodland, nearby scrub, meadows, lakes and reedbeds make this a treasure trove of bird, plants and insect life –

with no fewer than 26 species of butterfly.

The mature, open woods featuring large and splendid mature oaks contrast with denser younger woodland. Looking out you can enjoy views of the expansive mudflats and salt marshes of the Dyfi Estuary.

The peat bog is a scarce habitat and its resident plants – insectivorous sundews, bog asphodel, royal fern and rare bog rosemary – all the more precious.

Beside the paths bluebells, primroses, lords-and-ladies and anemones add their colour. Look above, too, for red kites, buzzards, peregrines and, in winter, redwings and white-fronted geese.

Ynys-hir

MAP 3

Tan y Coed
Corris

On the left as you drive along
A487 from Machynlleth to Corris.
(SH755053) 700ha (1730 acres)
Forestry Commission

Magnificent oak and beech
trees that have been allowed to
grow to maturity among the
conifers of this large, hilly
plantation add extra drama to
this quiet woodland.

Some parts of the plantation
have been thinned to provide
pretty views and, in another, an
attractive mountain stream runs
through, edged by ferns and
mosses. Elsewhere there are
more open woodland areas of
towering Douglas fir and at the
top you can enjoy wide views
of the surrounding hillsides,
cloaked in spruce, hemlock,
larch and fir.

In contrast, on the lower
slopes there are areas of native
broadleaf trees, including oak,
birch and rowan, with an
understorey of hazel and goat
willow. Open areas are full of
rosebay willow herb and
foxgloves.

A wide, forest track leads up
into the woods with several
steep and narrow paths
radiating off it – to be tackled
only by the reasonably fit.

Douglas fir cones

Abergynolwyn,
Coed Nant Gwernol,
Coed Hendrewallog
Abergynolwyn

From A487 Dolgellau to
Machynlleth road, take the B4405
to Tywyn. Park at the Canolfan in
Abergynolwyn. Walk up a steep
tarmac lane from the Canolfan,
entering Coed Nant Gwernol via a
public footpath on the right. Access
to these woods is also possible via
the Talyllyn Railway, a narrow gauge
line starting in Tywyn. (SH683063)
655 ha (1619acres)
Forestry Commission and
Woodland Trust

Dramatic scenery and the
sounds of water careering
down a boulder-strewn ravine
attack the senses in the
dramatic U-shaped glacial
valley of the Afon Dysynni.

The narrow pathway through
the wood follows the contour
of the valley, running parallel
with the stream. The sessile oak
woodland – a remnant of the
wild wood – has survived
perhaps because this narrow
ravine is too small to cultivate
or fell.

A junction to a bridge over
the gorge leads to the narrow
gauge railway terminus.
Continue through the wood
and another bridge takes you
into plantations managed by
the Forestry Commission. It is
possible to return via routes
on the other side of the valley,
or continue up past a view of
a waterfall and then climb out
of the valley and return to
Abergynolwyn either through
the new broadleaved
woodland of Coed
Hendrewallog or along the
tarmac lane higher up.

A leaflet describing walks
in some of the woods is
available locally.

Gold ringed dragon fly

Dyfi Forest
Machynlleth

From Machynlleth follow A487
north, then minor road right
through villages of Corris and
Aberllefenni. Follow road through
Dyfi Forest to Aberangell on the
east side where there are pull-ins
and places to park alongside road.
(SH783105) 6000 ha (14830 acres)
Forestry Commission

It's easy to lose yourself in
nature on a visit to Dyfi, a
massive conifer forest stretching
across endless acres of rolling
countryside.

It is possible to walk or cycle
for miles without seeing
another soul – and that makes
it a great place to enjoy
tranquillity and space to think.
But, despite a network of well-
marked tracks and paths, a
compass and map are
recommended as essential
companions.

Despite the dominance of
conifers, there are some
wonderful verdant oak woods
with mosses, bilberry and ferns
all dripping with moisture,
which lie on steep slopes, from
where you can enjoy wonderful
views across the forest canopy.

There are several old slate
mines in the area an old slate
trackway leads down by a big
bubbling stream. In the heart of
the forest are nothing but miles
of mature conifers and the
sound of rushing stream water.

Farchynys
Dollgellau

Follow A496 through Bontddu,
entrance and car park on left.
(SH663182)
Snowdonia National Park

Colossal oaks with massive
girths line the lower slopes of
this little island that divides a
road and a river estuary.

Rocky and isolated, the
woodland–swathed hillock rises
out of the marshes and
reedbeds of the estuary to
produce lush vegetation of
bramble, nettle and goat willow.

A pathway follows the
ancient, moss–covered stone
wall boundary of the wood at
the base of the hill. Small,
grassy paths lead off to the top
of the large rock. It's a steep
climb but well worth it when
you see the phenomenal views
over the Mawddach estuary.

The higher you climb, the
smaller the trees because of the
thinner soil. Some of the
birches have grown tall while

others have begun to die back,
providing a habitat for birch
polypore fungus.

At the end of the wide track,
a ladder stile leads to the
estuary marshes where reed
beds provide a habitat for
sedge, grasshopper warblers and
reed buntings.

Farchynys

MAP 3

Mawddach Woodlands
Dolgellau

A493, just outside Dolgellau, look out for George III Hotel. Park near the toll bridge on the right in Penmaenpool and walk up path to woodland (Coed Garth Gell). (SH688192) 523 ha (1292 acres)

RSPB

Some have said the spectacular views from the heather-covered summit of this hillside woodland are the best in Wales. The nightjars who nest here might agree.

This is a steep sessile oak wood with paths wending their way to the top. The first section of oak and the occasional birch gives way to beech as you follow the trail upwards. The steep valley straddles a noisy stream that feeds into the Mawddach.

Old stone walls dot the wood and the track appears ancient, with moss-covered stones. Nearer the top, ruined miners' buildings give a hint of its goldmine origins.

It is also possible to approach the summit by parking close to the Borthwnog Hall Hotel and walking back along the road to the entrance. The path is in good condition but becomes increasingly steep as you near the summit, which has spectacular views across the Mawddach estuary.

Mawddach Woodlands

Gaer Fawr

Gaer Fawr
Welshpool

From Welshpool take A490 north,
then B4392 northeast to Guilsfield
Cegidfa. Take last turning left out of
village up a hill. Wood on right,
with car park at end of wood.
(SJ222128) 30 ha (74 acres)
Woodland Trust

A local landmark and very
popular with local people, this
semi-natural woodland, much
of it ancient, lines the flanks of
a prominent hill, topped by an
impressive Iron Age hill fort.

The woodland, which is
relatively remote and partly
enclosed by historic boundary
hedgerows, is a special place
with a peaceful feel.

It's also a wood of great
beauty and in the spring,
carpets of bluebells line the
woodland floor.

Well managed and inviting, it
boasts a mixture of tree species
from dominant oak to birch,
hazel, cherry, ash, rowan,
sycamore, hawthorn and sallow.
Also present are less-common
trees such as wych elm, crab
apple, field maple and sweet
chestnut. Rockier, drier areas
support blackthorn, gorse
and broom.

Several well-marked pathways
ascend quite steeply up through
former oak coppice and stands
of mature oaks, leading
eventually to the well-preserved
ramparts of the fort, a scheduled
ancient monument.

MAP 3

Lake Vyrnwy Forest
Llanwddyn

From Welshpool take A458 west, then B4382 northwest. It is well signed.
(SH991223) 2,000 ha (5,000 acres) SSSI

Vyrnwy Partnership

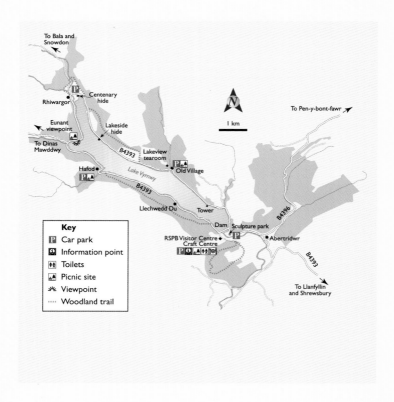

Key

P Car park
i Information point
†† Toilets
▲ Picnic site
✹ Viewpoint
···· Woodland trail

Lake Vyrnwy Dam

Vast, varied and stunning whatever the weather, it needs a full day to do justice to Lake Vyrnwy.

This is the land of the big conifer, with vast cloud-covered forests set around a massive, manmade reservoir and masses to do, from challenging walks and cycle trails to visitor facilities, bird hides and the assurance of access for all.

There are displays and leaflets to help you plan your route and a sculpture park with access for people in wheelchairs, along with an animal puzzle trail to ensure that the site truly offers something for everyone.

The lake was built to provide water for Liverpool and provides a beautiful focal point with endless miles of challenging and exhilarating forest track. A 12-mile circular walk is being created around the lake.

The large RSPB reserve in the Berwyn mountain foothills covers a wide range of habitats, with heather moorland, forests, meadows, mountain streams, rivers, waterfalls and crags.

The site includes nearly 500 acres of broadleaved woodland,

MAP 3

much of it sessile oak and some of it dating back to the Ice Age. Today it supports a rich mix of species.

Breeding birds include the pied flycatcher and wood warbler. Buzzards are frequently heard overhead while golden-ringed dragonfly can be seen darting about. In the autumn, hundreds of redwing and fieldfare arrive.

Just five miles south of Lake Vyrnwy is Dyfnant Forest, a large, predominately coniferous working forest with pockets of native broadleaves (Grid ref SJ033154). Interesting for its birdlife, you may glimpse a goshawk, which has become more widespread since the 1980s, crossbills and black grouse.

For contrast, try the small but rather lovely Coed Pendugwm. One mile north of Pontrobert (Grid ref SJ103142), you'll discover a 'wild wood' created by 400-year-old oaks and carpets of bluebells, wood anemones, primroses and violets beneath. Montgomeryshire Wildlife Trust, keepers of this eight-acre site, are custodians of a thriving colony of dormice. Park in the reserve car park opposite Pendugwm Farm.

Dormouse

Breidden Forest
Welshpool

From A458 east of Shrewsbury, take B4393. Breidden Hill is 6.5km (4 miles) on left with car park. (SJ299139) 262 ha (623 acres)
Forestry Commission

Breathtaking panoramic views of the countryside await the visitor to this mixed woodland site – provided you have the stamina to tackle a taxing hillside climb.

Following one of three walking routes through the woodland you will encounter a variety of species, including ash, birch, rowan and cherry, elm, beech and horse chestnut and honeysuckle clambering over young trees. Taller trees tower overhead as you make your way up the forest track.

There are open scree slopes with a mixture of tall herbs while pendulous sedge can be found in the wooded areas.

Occasionally a small path runs off the track and the wood opens out to provide a panorama of the surrounding landscape. If you have the grit and determination to get to the top the 360-degree vista is truly amazing.

Returning, it's important to follow the path back to the car park and not be tempted to take a short cut through the forest, because the hillside is precipitous.

Breidden Forest

MAP 4

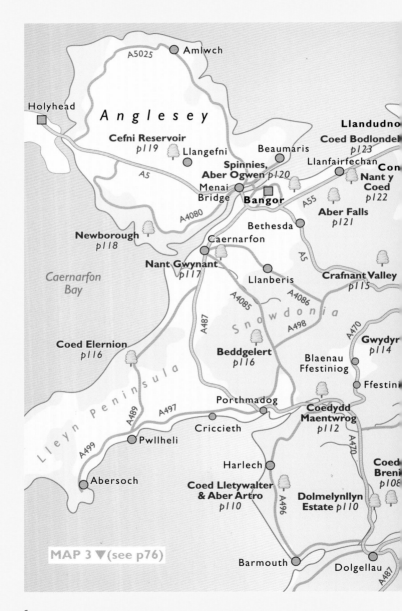

Amlwch

A5025

Holyhead

A n g l e s e y

Cefni Reservoir
p119

Llangefni

Beaumaris

Llandudno

Coed Bodlondeb
p123

Llanfairfechan

Con

A5

Spinnies,
Aber Ogwen *p120*

Menai
Bridge

Bangor

Nant y
Coed
p122

A55

Newborough
p118

A4080

Bethesda

Aber Falls
p121

Caernarfon

Nant Gwynant
p117

Llanberis

A5

Crafnant Valley
p115

Caernarfon
Bay

A4085

S n o w d o n i a

A4086

A498

Coed Elernion
p116

A487

Beddgelert
p116

Blaenau
Ffestiniog

A470

Gwydyr
p114

L l e y n   P e n i n s u l a

Porthmadog

Ffestin

A489

A497

Criccieth

Coedydd
Maentwrog
p112

A499

Pwllheli

Abersoch

Harlech

Coed
Breni
p108

A470

Coed Lletywalter
& Aber Artro
p110

A496

Dolmelynllyn
Estate *p110*

MAP 3 ▼(see p76)

Barmouth

Dolgellau

A487

106

Marl Hall
Woods p124
Bryn Euryn p125
Colwyn   Coed y Gopa p126
Bay
Pwllycrochan
Woods
p126   Abergele

Prestatyn
Rhyl

Wallasey
LIVERPOOL
Birkenhead

St Asaph

Holywell

Flint

Queensferry

Coed y Felin
Hendre p130

Denbigh

Moel Fammau
Country Park
p129

Mold

nrwst

Coed Hafod p114
etws-
coed

Clocaenog
Forest p127

Ruthin

Coed
Cilygroeslwyd
p128

Wrexham

Wrexham
Country Parks
p132

Erddig
Country
Park
p130

Pen y Coed p134   Ruabon

Llangollen

Bala

Coed Collfryn p135

N

Oswestry

10 miles

10 km

wyd

MAP 4

Coed y Brenin
Dolgellau
Signposted on A470 north of Dolgellau. Drive through wood to reach car park. (SH752251) 3000 ha (7413acres)
Forestry Commission

Key

P Car park
ℹ️ Information point
🚻 Toilets
⛱ Picnic site
🌿 Viewpoint
▦ Woodland trail
🚲 Mountain biking

Coed y Brenin – Wood of the King – is indeed, fit for a king, with thousands of acres of Forest Park covering the valleys of the Mawddach, Eden, Wen and Gain.

The site was, in fact, once part of the Nannau estate belonging to Cadougan, Prince of Powys, around 1100 AD. Today the site is mainly coniferous with some broadleaf areas and much of the plantation is managed for landscape. That means there are lots of areas of mature Douglas fir, Scots pine and larch that are a pleasure to walk and cycle through.

This site is a treasure trove of leisure activities and considered the finest mountain biking territory in the UK. Enthusiasts are well catered for, with cycle hire facilities on site.

There are three waymarked trails, aimed at both novices and experts, and onsite cycle-hire facilities leave no excuse for not getting to grips with the sporting experience.

There are also two orienteering course routes.

One is designed for families while the other, open to all, is used regularly for international competitions.

A new state-of-the-art visitor centre opened in 2006, with a range of facilities to complement the mainly coniferous woodland of mature Douglas fir, Scots pine and larch.

There is also some broadleaved woodland, particularly around the plantation edges and rivers as well as open heather heathland, craggy hilltops, meadows, river valleys and waterfalls to discover. It may be a vast site but don't forget to look at detail such as the texture and colour of mosses and lichen which add interest at a much smaller-scale.

Also waiting to be discovered are activity play areas for the children, nature pond, copper and gold mines, and some splendid examples of mature conifers, planted in 1923.

Four waymarked routes, graded for difficulty, guide the visitor to the most picturesque streams and viewpoints.

MAP 4

Dolymellyn Estate
Dolgellau

5km (3 miles) north of Dolgellau
on A470 you reach the small
village of Ganllwyd. Car park on
right in village. (SH726245)
485 ha (1,200 acres)
National Trust

Within the estate lies a
dramatic Atlantic oak
woodland that is designated a
National Nature Reserve.

It looks – at first sight –
slightly out of character with
the steep-sided valley and the
conifer plantations that rise
from the riverbanks and up the
sides of the steep, craggy hills.

On-site information panels
guide the visitor by the River
Gamian waterfalls at Rhaider
Du and a disused goldmine
that stands at the top of the
site. Look out for insectivorous
butterwort that grows in the
damp but infertile soils. Pied
flycatchers can also be seen in
the oak woods.

A short walk down the hill
leads to the boulder-dotted
River Mawddach, which carves
its way through the bedrock to
the Vast Mawddach estuary a
few miles downstream.

Alder, birch, ash and oak
grow in these slightly more
fertile damp soils where ferns,
mosses and liverworts thrive in
the humid conditions.

Coed Lletywalter & Coed Aber Artro
Harlech

From Llanbedr on A496 take
minor road towards Cwm Bychan.
Coed Lletywalter is on the left
shortly after passing a junction on
the right. There is a gateway and
enough space to park a single car
without blocking the entrance. For
Coed Aber Artro turn right at the
previous junction, over a stone
bridge, then almost immediately
cross another bridge on a bend.

The road soon enters the
woodland. Park on verges just off
road within wood.
(Coed Lletywalter SH599276)
(Coed Aber Artro SH599268)
65 ha (161acres) SSSI
Woodland Trust

These two adjoining sites
create great atmosphere.
Mosses and liverworts thrive in
the damp climate of Coed

Lletywalter's oak-dominated woodland, while beech is the main player in parts of Coed Aber Artro.

Rocky outcrops punctuate the sites, moistened by regular rainfall and water that runs through. Bilberry and fern grow here in profusion.

A torrential river, the Afon Cwmnantcol, rushes from the 700m-high mountains of Rhinog Fawr and Rhinog Fach to the sea, passing through the narrow valley where Coed Aber Artro lies. A small dam is worth seeking out to witness the impressive overflow of white water falling to the valley floor below while a lake lies at the heart of Coed Lletywalter.

A relatively level and easy footpath leads around Coed Lletywalter and a pleasant, circular walk on stony paths can be enjoyed through Coed Aber Artro.

Coed Aber Artro

MAP 4

Coedydd Maentwrog
Penrhydeudraeth

Centered around the Plas Tan y Bwlch Field Studies Centre at Maentwrog
a few miles east of Penrhydeudraeth. (SH655408)

1,000+ ha (2,500+ acres) SSSI

Various owners

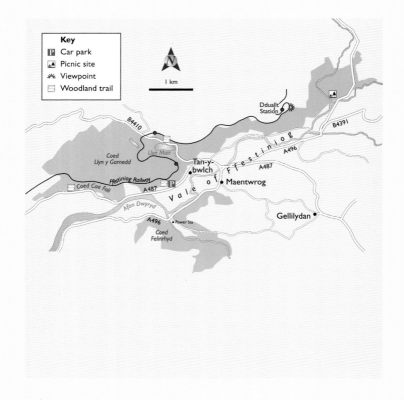

This truly beautiful collection of woodlands lines the sides of the Vale of Ffestiniog at the point where the steep gorge that cuts through the stunning Snowdonia mountains begins to widen.

North and south are heather-clad craggy mountains while westward the softer, rolling landscape stretches out to the sand dunes of Tremadog Bay.

The natural part of the wood is upland oak; the year-round humidity sustains a wealth of lichens, mosses and liverworts. During the 18th and 19th centuries, nature's work was improved upon with the addition of a lake, bridges, paths and viewpoints to help visitors enjoy this stunning countryside.

Wildlife abounds in the shape of pied flycatchers, jays, buzzards, dragonflies, butterflies and wildflowers.

Woods include:

Coed Felinrhyd, on the south side of the valley, is mainly ancient upland oak with some conifers, which you can explore on a circular walk alongside a fast-flowing stream. Mosses and ferns thrive and you can enjoy splendid mountain views.

Plas Tan y Bwlch, is a national park study centre, with landscaped woodland, rocky outcrops and luxuriant exotic trees and shrubs.

Coed Hafod y Llyn is upland oak woodland overlooking the lake, Llyn Mair, a favourite haunt of dippers, tits, nuthatches and creepers, while **Coed Llyn Mair** is an excellent upland Atlantic oak woodland with small mountain streams and ancient, twisted oaks.

Coed Camlyn This is a beautiful wooded hillside overlooking the Vale of Ffestiniog and a national nature reserve because of the abundance of rare lichens, liverworts and mosses. This is also the European stronghold of the lesser horseshoe bat.

Coed Cymerau Isaf, near Blaenau Festiniog, is oak woodland, meadows and wetlands. The site is peaceful and gently undulating with some boggy fields and woodland of oak, ash, birch and hazel coppice.

A leaflet is available locally which describes waymarked walks in some of the woods.

MAP 4

Gwydyr
Betws y Coed
Start at Betws y Coed, there are
numerous entrances. (SH777509)
10,000 ha (25,000 acres)
Forestry Commission

Dubbing Gwydyr a 25,000-acre
playground would be telling
just half the story.

It provides employment for
many local people and offers
peace and tranquillity for
hundreds of visitors.

Gwydyr has much to offer the
adventurer in the shape of
mountain streams, torrential
falls, reservoirs, broadleaved
woodlands, boulder-strewn

rivers, pine forests, rocky crags
and cliff edges.

Little wonder this forest park,
replanted with oak, beech, larch
and Douglas and silver fir, is
enjoyed by millions each year
who come to walk, cycle,
canoe, fish, orienteer and climb.

The vast site enfolds the busy
tourist town of Betws y Coed
and has been forested since the
last Ice Age, though the original
wild woods are long gone.

For three centuries this was a
busy mining area and the
industrial heritage is still in
evidence, with mine shafts,
engine houses, reservoirs and,
most usefully, old miners'
tracks which today provide
excellent access.

Coed Hafod
Betws y Coed
1.5km (1 mile) from Betws y Coed
on A470 toward Llanrwst,
woodland on right just after
Drapers Field Studies Centre on
left. (SH808577) 22 ha (54 acres)
Snowdonia National Park

Bats and woodpeckers thrive in
this oak-dominated ancient
woodland, thanks to abundant

deadwood habitats, which
support a healthy insect
population.

The site is relatively dry, so
lacks the ferns and mosses
found in nearby humid woods
by lakes and streams. However,
moss covers the rocky outcrops
of the wood's upper sections,
from where there are good
views down into the Conwy
valley and the woodlands
beyond.

Bluebells proliferate in

sections along with dog's mercury, strawberry, herb Robert and enchanter's nightshade. Trees include hazel, birch, holly and young ash.

Peaceful and undisturbed, the site is explored via a circular, well-made path but you need to be relatively fit to tackle the steeper sections leading to areas of rocky outcrops and ruined farmsteads.

Busy Betws y Coed is nearby with its many attractions.

Crafnant Valley
Trefriw

Turn left at Trefriw on B5106, signposted Llyn Crafnant. (SH740610) 1260 ha (3114 acres)
Forestry Commission

Like a spider emerging from a bath's plughole, the drive into this mixed woodland site emerges after a steep climb between narrow valley sides to reveal a vast lake surrounded by tree-clad mountains.

Set at more than 390ft above sea level, the site, known as the 'Lake in the Valley of Garlic', is home to the UK's smallest bird, the goldcrest, as well as dippers, mallards, great-crested grebes, buzzards and coal tits.

There is a three-mile walk around the lake, which is relatively easy to tackle, and many walks along wide forest tracks to viewpoints and vistas across the lake towards Snowdon and the Glyders.

Smaller paths dip into the woods where pine, larch, hemlock and spruce grow between moss-covered boulders and rocky outcrops.

The paucity of the soil means trees tend to be sparse, producing a light, open feel to the wood. Selective felling has also taken place to great effect as it has opened up the views.

Crafnant Valley

MAP 4

Beddgelert Forest
Beddgelert

North of the village of Beddgelert
on the A4085. (SH562497)
1,000 ha (2,500 acres)
Forestry Commission

Packed with facilities and
hugely popular, this Forestry
Commission holiday centre site
has ample room for all.

Set in a relatively level, wide
valley with three or four rocky
headlands jutting into the
forest.

Most of the woodland is
coniferous, with some
magnificent specimens planted
in the 1920s, and broadleaves
adding variety along the
woodland edges.

There is a small lake, with
streams feeding into the fast-
flowing, foaming river. A bridge
provides a safe vantage point.

There is an excellent
numbered waymarker scheme
to help visitors negotiate the
web of paths – but a map is
always a good idea. The wide
forest tracks provide easy
walking but these can
occasionally get steep.

There is plenty of interest
not far from the car park, with
conifers, oak, ash, sycamore,
birch and hazel, easy walking
and a torrential stream just
minutes away. Those who
climb the headland, however,
are rewarded with stunning
views.

Coed Elernion
Trefor

From A487 Cernarfon – Pwllheli
road turn into the more southerly
minor road to Trefor. Wood is on
left. (SH378460)
20 ha (50 acres) AONB SSSI
Woodland Trust

Here is a wood to head for if
you like your countryside quiet,
remote and undisturbed – and
particularly pleasing on the eye.

This site offers a real variety of
habitats – woodland, scrub,
grassland and streams all set on
gently sloping ground. As it can
be wet in places you are advised
to wear wellies.

Although remote, is worth a
visit to enjoy its abundance of
bluebells, delightful grassland
and numerous butterflies, birds
and bats.

A mix of well-established, mature woodland and more recently developed woods, along with wet alder and willow-dominated sections and drier areas of oak, birch and ash, the site also features long-established fields where swathes of yellow rattle provide an attractive summer feature.

To the east is marshy grassland dominated by purple moor-grass, sharp-flowered rush and giant horsetail. Active management is controlling birch and gorse from encroaching on species-rich areas.

Nant Gwynant
Beddgelert

Park at the Bethania car park in Nan Gwynant on the A498. Wood is on opposite side of road from car park. (SH505625)
30 ha (74 acres)
National Trust

There cannot be a better place to experience the true rugged wild wood that once clothed most of Wales than these superb Atlantic oak and ash woodlands on Snowdon's rocky foothills.

This is a damp, humid environment, with water racing down mountain streams, evaporating from the lake or hanging in the air as mist. Every tree, rock and piece of earth is coated with mosses or lichens. So rich is the population of mosses, liverworts and ferns that the sites have been designated of international importance.

Most of the woodland is oak, with some birch and ash on the lower slopes. The dramatic location makes you marvel at the tenacity of the twisted oaks to survive such a hostile environment.

From within the wood you can enjoy stunning views of the lake, Llyn Gwynant and of course, Snowdon itself. Access is good but the steep, narrow paths can be slippery so caution is needed.

MAP 4

Newborough Forest
Newborough

Village of Newborough is at the end of B4421. Follow road signposted Llys Rhosyr to access forest. (SH403654)
8700 ha (21,500 acres)
Forestry Commission

The rare sight of red squirrels could await you in this vast seaside plantation on Anglesey's southwest coast, where the threatened native still has a stronghold.

The peninsula features Corsican, lodge pole and Scots pines planted on the edge of popular beaches.

The site consists mainly of sand dunes, and there are some rocky outcrops and small cliffs. You can walk for miles exploring the site and through to the rocky island of Llanddwyn, with its ruined church and lighthouse.

There are two waymarked routes – a one-mile trail through sheltered pines where, in summer, the rare crossbill can be seen. Look too for the quaintly named viper's bugloss and evening primrose growing

Newborough Forest

beside the track.

The other trail, which takes you along wide forest tracks, is ideal for families. Species to look out for include the tiny goldcrest, ravens, sparrow hawks and coal tits along with peacock, common blue and meadow brown butterflies.

Cefni Reservoir
Llangefni

From the village of Llangefni take B5111. Car park on left alongside conifer plantation. Look out for brown Nature Reserve road sign. (SH436773) 77 ha (190 acres)

Forestry Commission/Dwr Cymry

This pleasant conifer plantation, set around a large reservoir, is a good location to walk the dog, enjoy a picnic or walk around the water.

Most of the trees are close-grown Norway and Sitka spruce. The dense canopy allows in little light so there are very few plants beneath.

However, there is a good population of birds here, thanks in the main to the variety of habitats provided by the reservoir – along with the shelter and security that the site provides.

Keep your eyes open for willow warbler, white throat, song thrush and chaffinch, to name but a few.

Nearer the water are broadleaves, such as goat willow, alder and birch. Look out for red admiral butterflies, along with peacock, small copper and speckled wood and in summer, dragonflies darting about.

A network of paths gives level, if occasionally slippery, access around the site.

MAP 4

Spinnies, Aberogwen Reserve
Bangor

From A55 take A5 signed Penrhyn Castle. Follow minor road to Tal y Bont then signs for nature reserve. Car park at end of road.
(SH613721) 4 ha (10 acres)
North Wales Wildlife Trust

Birdwatchers should make a beeline for this site, which lies just inland from the mudflats on the Menai estuary.

The woodland is level, fertile and moist with a small lake in the middle and several small islands and bird hides, making it ideal to view a variety of species.

Look out for sedge warblers, chiffchaff, mallard, moorhen, bullfinch, black cap, redshank, kingfisher, grey heron, lapwing and curlew… to name but a few of the breeds the site supports, thanks to the mix of wetland, woodland and open water.

The woodland itself is a complete contrast from the upland woods of Gwynedd, being a mix of oak, ash, sycamore, elder, alder, hazel, aspen and Scots pine, including many fine specimens.

Well-surfaced, easy, waymarked paths provide a clear route for walkers – entrance is at the end of a 10ft-high stone wall, part of the Penrhyn Castle estate. The path and main hide are accessible by wheelchairs.

Spinnies, Aberogwen Reserve

Aber Falls
Abergwyngregyn

Turn off J13 A55 between Bangor
and Llanfairfechan, signposted
Abergwyngregyn. Follow uphill
road from village then follow signs.
(SH671710) 140 ha (346 acres)
**Countryside Council for Wales
and Forestry Commission**

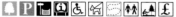

Lying on the valley of the Afon
Rhaeadr fawr, with the steepest
river gradient in England and
Wales, the 'star' of Aber Falls
wood is a stunning 300ft
waterfall.

Birdsong and the sound of the
mountain stream flowing over
huge boulders are the only
noises to break the silence in
this steep-sided ancient
woodland of oak, ash and alder.

There is plenty to see and
enjoy as you wind your way
along the mile-long route, via
an occasionally steep path, to
the falls.

Rare lichens clad the ancient
woodland trees and in spring,
the goshawk can be spotted in
the skies overhead and pied
flycatchers come to breed in
the wood. Look out too for
blackcaps, redstarts and
bullfinch and, occasionally,
choughs, peregrines, ravens
and buzzards.

Sheep are common in the
upland areas and feral ponies
graze the hillsides. Near the top
is a small visitor's centre with
details of man's 3,000-year
relationship with this very
special valley.

Aber Falls

MAP 4

Nant y Coed
Llanfairfechan

Turn off A55 to Llanfairfechan,
11km (7 miles) west of Conwy. At
traffic lights on Village Road turn
left into Valley Road and straight
up Newry Drive. Parking on
hairpin bend. (SH697738)
9ha (22 acres)

Conwy County Borough Council

The sounds of the Afon Ddu
rushing down the
mountainside to the sea
accompany an otherwise
peaceful walk through this
compact wooded valley.

Squeezed between the
mountains and the sea, the site
was popular in Victorian times,
as its well-worn stepping
stones testify. Rocks and fast
streams blend with twisted
upland oak woods to lend a
naturally rugged appeal.

Little bridges, flights of steps
and footbridges make a walk
around the wood very pleasant
indeed and a walk up the
steeper section is rewarded
with fine views to Anglesey.

Woodland flowers such as
cuckoo pint, bluebell, anemone
and wood sorrel thrive here
beneath rowan, hazel, wild
cherry, alder, ash, beech and
sycamore, while on the rocky
hillside is an oak upland wood
with patches of heather and
bilberry.

Ferns abound anywhere the
air is damp and mosses thrive
on the rocks along the water's
edge. Look out for glimpses of
redstart, pied flycatchers, grey
wagtail, buzzards and dippers.

Coed Bodlondeb

Coed Bodlondeb
Conwy

Walk from Conwy Castle along
Marine Walk skirting the bay to
wooded promontory jutting into
the estuary. (SH778781)
8 ha (20 acres)
Conwy County Borough Council

A stone's throw from the
popular tourist attractions at
Conwy, this site is the perfect
way to introduce young family
members to the magic of
woodland.

It takes just half an hour to
tour the wood, planted in the
18th century when it was
called Welsh Arcadia. The one-
mile route leads from the castle
right into the woodland which
is made up of a variety of trees
and shrubs, both native and
exotic, including magnificent
beech, sycamore, holly, oak,
silver birch, Scots pine, cedar,
lime and copper beech.

Flowering plants such as
gorse, foxglove, rosebay willow
herb and woodsage grow
around a house that dates back
to 1877.

Visitors can enjoy enviable
views over the estuary to the
Great Orme, the castle, the
Conwy Valley, Puffin Island
and Anglesey.

MAP 4

Marl Hall Woods
Llandudno junction

Take A470 signed Llandudno off
A55. Turn right off second
roundabout into Marl Lane.
(SH799788) 12 ha (30 acres) SSSI
Woodland Trust

This site may be relatively
small, but it's high enough to
be seen for miles around,
particularly the limestone
outcrops at the top.

An ancient woodland site,
Marl Hall Woods are an
important feature in the
Conwy valley and well used by
local residents.

The lower slopes were
extensively replanted in the
1960s with beech and conifers
and now support mature
exotics such as Norway maple,
lime, horse chestnut, sweet
chestnut, poplar, pine and
larch.

Higher slopes are dominated
by oak, ash, wych elm and yew.
There are some planted
species, though many are being
removed to encourage a return
to ash woodland. The flower-
rich grassland at the top
supports nationally scarce
species.

Diverse though sparse, the

Marl Hall Woods

shrub layer includes hazel, holly, elder, spindle and spurge laurel. Carpets of ivy dominate the woodland floor along with hart's-tongue fern, male fern, wood melick and the nationally scarce ivy broomrape.

Bryn Euryn
Colwyn Bay

Take B5115 off A55, signed Rhos on Sea. At first roundabout head straight on for Llandudno and follow brown tourist signs to Bryn Euryn. The site is visible from afar as a wooded area on high ground. (SH831798) 25 ha (62 acres) SSSI
Conway County Council

This isolated limestone hill overlooking Colwyn Bay has been a strategic viewpoint for hundreds of years.

On it stands a 6th-century hill fort and a ruined three-storey 15th-century mansion, with glorious views across the bay and the miles of wooded countryside beyond.

The hillside woods, with their rocky outcrops, include some unusual trees, including spurge laurel and spindle. Limestone soils support an attractive mix of flora, with kidney vetch, rockrose, lady's bedstraw, carline thistle, yellow wort, salad burnet and wild thyme. In the shallow soils nationally scarce hoary rockrose and Nottingham catchfly grow, as do early purple, pyramidal and green-winged orchids.

The paths can be steep but the mile-long circular walk is not too taxing.

An open grassy area alongside the car park is full of insect life in summer, including the six-spotted burnet moth and up to 26 different butterfly species. Wild clematis festoons the vertical slabs of rock.

MAP 4

Pwllycrochan Woods
Colwyn Bay

Uphill out of Colwyn Bay, through a residential area, you reach the Old Highway. This runs along the bottom of the wood and there is an entrance opposite Pwllycrochan Avenue where parking is advised. (SH842784) 21 ha (52 acres)
Conway County Council

If you ever holiday in Colwyn Bay, this peaceful woodland is well worth a visit, as it forms the southerly backdrop to the seaside town.

The ancient woodland sections of the site include oak, hazel, holly, wych elm, birch and elder. The rest is planted Scot pine, yew, larch, beech, sweet chestnut and Cyprus fir. Together, they sustain a variety of wildlife which thrives here.

Exotic shrubs, including snowberry, flowering nutmeg and pheasant berry, can be spotted. More aggressive species such as rhododendron and laurel are gradually being removed.

Steep in places, the paths follow the contours of the valley, out of which colossal beech trees rise up. Some of the older trees have been retained to sustain insects, which in turn provide food for nuthatches and woodpeckers. Tawny owls nest in the rotten hollows. Bluebells, wood anemone, dog's mercury and wood sorrel bloom here in spring.

Coed y Gopa
Abergele

From Abergele take B5443 westwards, following signs for golf club. Past golf club, turn right and continue up hill. Small parking area at main entrance 200m on left. (SH937767)
47 ha (116 acres) SSSI
Woodland Trust

A deep, narrow gorge and natural caves in the limestone hills southwest of Abergele provide an important winter hibernation base for the lesser horseshoe bat. That's why the woodland is designated a Site of Special Scientific Interest (SSSI).

And there is much more than first meets the eye in this mixed forest, some of which is planted beech, pine and larch on an ancient woodland site.

Sections have been thinned to allow the regeneration of native broadleaves and elsewhere are small areas of species-rich limestone grassland with crested hair-grass, quaking-grass, common rock rose and mouse-ear hawkweed.

There are a number of points where spectacular views over Abergele and the North Wales coast can be gained and a walk to the top of the site takes you to the remains of an Iron Age hill fort, now a Scheduled Ancient Monument.

The site is crossed by wide tracks and open rides, suitable for most abilities although not wheelchairs. Some can become slippery so explore with care.

Clocaenog Forest
Ruthin
The B5105 passes right through the forest. There are several small car parks, the best being Bod Petrual just south of the road. (SJ027542) 400 ha (990 acres)
Forestry Commission

You could spend weeks exploring the miles of paths that criss-cross through this large forest site. But only proficient map-readers should try – since there are no waymarked trails or leaflets available.

Navigation problems aside, this is a gently undulating plantation of 55-year-old Sitka spruce with a good network of tracks, where the native red squirrel has been able to regain the upper hand, thanks to the well-thinned conifers.

Black grouse is another rare species in Wales that is being actively encouraged in the ▶▶

Clocaenog Forest

MAP 4

forest, through the constant creation of young heather growth for food, and conifer planting to provide their favourite habitat.

Bilberry, wood sorrel and heather thrive in the naturally acidic conditions of the clearing. In autumn there's a variety of fungi to discover, including fly agaric, amethyst deceiver and puffball. Look out too for brown hares, snipe, red grouse and adders.

Coed Cilygroeslwyd
Pwll-glas

A494 from Ruthin to Bala, at edge of Pwll-glas village, look for walking man sign into wood on right. Turn left down lane toward Llanfair and park just over river, bridge on left. Take care crossing road on way back to wood. (SJ124555)
4 ha (10 acres) SSSI
North Wales Wildlife Trust

Polecats make their home within this compact ancient woodland site, the only ash-yew woodland in Clwyd on limestone pavement

Lining the gently sloping valley of the Afon Clwyd, the reserve has much to intrigue, not least its rich mix of species which includes cranesbill and crosswort, wild daffodil and columbine, earth star, parasol and shaggy fungi, not to mention limestone woundwort – this is one of only two sites in Britain where it grows – and 30 different bird species.

The path leading into the reserve is lined with large oaks with mossy shoulders and ivy-draped ash trees. Limestone rocks like gravestones lend a churchyard feel as you walk through a dark yew tunnel which then opens up to reveal sunny grassland patches with many rare and beautiful plants – they include sweet woodruff, yellow archangel, sanicle, sweet violet, nettle-leaved bellflower and stinking hellebore.

The site is quite level but the circular walk can be narrow and slippery.

Moel Fammau Country Park
Llanbedr Dyffryn-Clwyd

From Ruthin take A494 toward Mold. In Llanbedr Dyffryn-Clwyd turn left up minor road (not B5429) which climbs and snakes across common to car park. (SJ170618) 600 ha (1483acres) AONB

Forestry Commission and Denbighshire County Council

Magnificent views across the Vale of Clywd – including Snowdon, Tryfan, Clogaenog Forest, Ruthin and Cader Idris – await you at the top of the Clwydian Range.

This heather-covered moorland was once totally wooded. Today there are still native broadleaves along the forest edges but most is larch, spruce and fir with some beech and red oak.

There are three hill forts in the area and it's worth making a beeline for the Jubilee Tower on the tallest hill, Moel Fammau, where the views are truly panoramic. Lemon-scented mountain fern can be found alongside the paths.

There are several walking routes. These can involve a steep climb through conifers to open heathland with carpets of bilberry, bramble, wood sorrel and heather, favoured by the red grouse.

Coed Ceunant, a broadleaved woodland in the valley below, is tricky to reach but great for visitors who enjoy a peaceful walk.

MAP 4

Coed y Felin
Hendre
Take A541 from Mold toward St
Asaph. Just before entering village
of Hendre follow sign to right for
Coed y Felin. Car park on left.
(SJ196677) (wheelchair access
SJ191677) 11ha (27 acres)
North Wales Wildlife Trust

A disused railway line – once
serving Mold to Denbigh and
closed in 1968, provides an
interesting and relatively easy
walk through a dense broadleaf
mix of oak and birch, ash,
sycamore, beech and the
occasional sweet chestnut.

From the main car park, a
short section of wildflower
grassland leads to a section of
elder, hazel, dog rose, holly,
wych elm and young ash. Dog's
mercury and ivy cover the
woodland floor which is
carpeted with bluebells in
spring.

As the mossy stone-wall-lined
path widens it heads down the
slope to meet a level gravel path
running on the woodland
bottom where sweet chestnut,
mosses and ferns thrive.

Several smaller paths and
public rights of way radiate into
the woodland, passing an old
lime tree, a fenced-off mine
shaft and several ruined stone
structures.

To protect the rich woodland
flora – this is the only site in
North Wales which boasts the
Deptford Pink, visitors are asked
to keep to paths, particularly in
spring and summer, and to keep
dogs on leads.

Erddig Country Park
Erdigg
On the A483, heading north
towards Wrexham, take A5152
signposted Erddig. Turn right off
A5152 signed Erddig onto minor
road. (SJ328485)
490 ha (1,200 acres)
National Trust

Britain's most important 18th
century walled garden lies
within this expansive and
beautiful parkland – home to
rare apple varieties, a canal pond
and national ivy collection.

The site stretches over acres of
woodland and parkland, with
meadow walks, water features
and streams.

You have a choice of routes to

explore, taking you past
fountains and cascades along
with an earlier earthwork
embankment known as
Wat's Dyke.

Hafod wood is a 172-acre wet
woodland with ash, alder,
willow and oak. The Black
Brook meanders through where
the spring flora is dominated by
white flowering Ransoms.

A block of beech, called Bryn
Golau, is perfect for autumn
fungus forays.

In the parkland you will find
some fine specimen trees and
veteran ash, sycamore, beech,
lime sequoia and oak –
forming a superb setting for the
main house.

Erddig Country Park

MAP 4

Wrexham Country Parks
Wrexham

On the outskirts of Wrexham, follow signs. Maps available from the council. (SJ289501) 20-160 ha (50–400 acres) SSSI

Wrexham County Borough Council

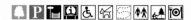

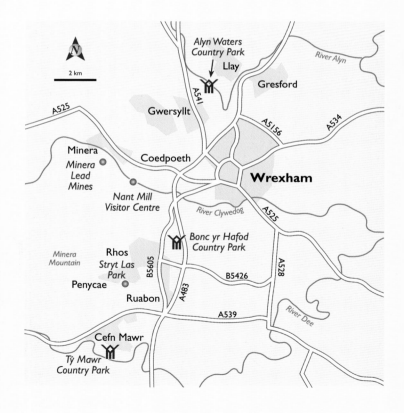

There are no fewer than six country parks on the west side of Wrexham, offering plenty of varied woodland to explore.

Nant Mill is a 72-acre site running alongside the river Clywedog. Partly ancient woodland, some of the oak and beech trees are more than 200 years old.

The wood was planted in the last three centuries with laurel, rhododendron and some conifers. Waterfalls and weirs were also added. Follow the generally easy paths high up along the valley side to enjoy a squirrel's eye view of the small, well-thinned fir plantation. Nant Mill adjoins Woodland Trust-owned Plas Power Woods

The wooded valley of the River Dee - **Ty Mawr Country Park** – passes beneath an imposing 147ft-high railway viaduct and the 120ft aqueduct build by Thomas Telford in 1805 – a unique woodland feature.

Stryt Las Country Park, dominated by wetland, with areas of open water and some woodland, is renowned for its population of great-crested newts.

Disused lead mines bear testimony to the industrial heritage of **Minera Country Park**. The path follows the old railway line to a disused limestone quarry with a spectacular lime kiln. Look out for some unusual plants.

A former landfill site and gravel pits have been re-landscaped to form a 400 acre park, **Alyn Waters**, which is a mass of young birch, ash, oak, willow, shrubs and mature trees line the river. Resident here are skylarks, broomrape and bee orchids.

Bonc yr Hafod was once a coal mine. Now it is planted with trees and a one-time spoil tip is a wooded hill overlooking the Welsh borders, with views that stretch as far as Liverpool.

Ty Mawr Country Park

Pen y Coed

Pen y Coed
Llangollen

In Llangollen follow signs for 'Youth Hostel' on A5. Just before hostel a public footpath (old trackway) leads off to right. You need to park elsewhere and walk back to this point and walk up hill into wood. (SJ227413) 28 ha (69 acres)
Woodland Trust

Providing a peaceful contrast to the bustle of nearby Llangollen, this mixed conifer and broadleaved woodland occupies a prominent hill overlooking the town.

Its position provides some excellent views across this pretty tourist spot and the surrounding countryside, including the craggy ridges of the Eglwyseg Escarpment and Castell Dinas Bran.

The start of the woodland walk is lined with conifers plus some birch and sycamore but interest soon deepens with more broadleaf trees, principally ash and oak. On leaving Pen y Coed the path dips back down the slope where woodland then opens into a beautiful grassy knoll dotted with old oaks, devil's-bit scabious, golden rod and wood sage growing among rocky wall remnants.

Continue on the path and drop into town or head south and re-enter Pen y Coed and explore further the diversity of old broadleaves and planted conifers together with its historic trackways and boundary walls.

On the southern side of the wood, sheep pasture is dotted with spectacular conifers and other parkland trees.

Coed Collfryn
Chirk

Turn off A5 at Chirk onto B4500, a scenic drive that's well worth taking. Turn left in Dol y Wern up a minor road, wood on your right. (SJ218370) 7 ha (17 acres)

Woodland Trust

A block of oak-dominated woodland occupying a hillside within the beautiful Ceiriog Valley, this was dubbed by Lloyd George as 'a little bit of heaven on earth'.

Tall, straight oaks are interspersed with the occasional cherry, ash and sycamore. Beside the rides, maple, rowan and holly grow and there is an understorey of honeysuckle and hazel, with cow-wheat and mosses cladding the woodland floor.

This is a well-thinned woodland with a network of paths which provide some fantastic views of the rolling landscape with its sheep-grazed pastures, low-clipped hedgerows, veteran trees and narrow country lanes.

The vista of the long, deep valley is dotted with small villages and houses. Along the route are a host of stunning features, including the world's highest boat ride – a viaduct and aqueduct built by Thomas Telford to take the Llangollen canal, now in line to become a World Heritage Site.

Coed Collfryn

WOODLAND
TRUST

Trees and forests are crucial to life on our planet. They generate oxygen, play host to a spectacular variety of wildlife and provide us with raw materials and shelter. They offer us tranquillity, inspire us and refresh our souls.

Founded in 1972, the Woodland Trust is now the UK's leading woodland conservation charity. By acquiring sites and campaigning for woodland it aims to conserve, restore and re-establish native woodland to its former glory. The Trust now owns and cares for over 1,100 woods throughout the UK.

The Woodland Trust wants to see:
no further loss of ancient woodland
the variety of woodland wildlife restored and improved
an increase in new native woodland
an increase in people's understanding and enjoyment of woodland

The Woodland Trust has 150,000 members who share this vision. For every new member, the Trust can care for approximately half an acre of native woodland. For details of how to join the Woodland Trust please either ring FREEPHONE 0800 026 9650 or visit the website at www.woodland-trust.org.uk.

If you have enjoyed the woods in this book please consider leaving a legacy to the Woodland Trust. Legacies of all sizes play an invaluable role in helping the Trust to create new woodland and secure precious ancient woodland threatened by development and destruction. For further information please either call 01476 581129 or visit our dedicated website at www.legacies.org.uk

Coed Collfryn

Further Information

Public transport

Each entry gives a brief description of location, nearest town and grid reference. Traveline provides impartial journey planning information about all public transport services either by ringing 0870 608 2608 (calls charged at national rates) or by visiting www.traveline.org.uk. For information about the Sustrans National Cycle Network either ring 0117 929 0888 or visit www.sustrans.org.uk

Useful contacts

Forestry Commission, 0845 367 3787, www.forestry.gov.uk
National Trust, 0870 458 4000, www.nationaltrust.org.uk
Wildlife Trusts, 0870 036 7711, www.wildlifetrusts.org
RSPB, 01767 680551, www.rspb.org.uk
Royal Forestry Society, 01442 822028, www.rfs.org.uk
Tree Council, 020 7407 9992, www.treecouncil.org.uk
Countryside Council for Wales, 0845 130 6229, www.ccw.gov.uk
Woodland Trust, 01476 581111, www.woodland–trust.org.uk

Recommend a Wood

You can play a part in helping us complete this series. We are inviting readers to nominate a wood or woods they think should be included. We are interested in any woodland with public access in England, Scotland, Wales and Northern Ireland.

To recommend a wood please photocopy this page and provide as much of the following information as possible:

About the wood

Name of wood: _____

Nearest town: _____

Approximate size: _____ ha/acres

Owner/manager: _____

A few words on why you think it should be included:

_____

_____

About you

Your name: _____

Your postal address: _____

_____

_____ Post code: _____

If you are a member of the Woodland Trust please provide your membership number.

Please send to: Exploring Woodland Guides, The Woodland Trust, Autumn Park, Dysart Road, Grantham, Lincolnshire NG31 6LL, by fax on 01476 590808 or e-mail woodlandguides@woodland-trust.org.uk

Thank you for your help

Other Guides in the Series

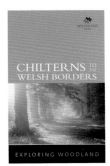

Chilterns to the
Welsh Borders

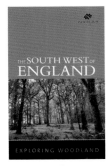

The South West
of England

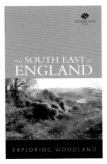

The South East
of England

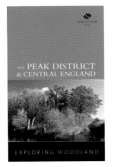

The Peak District
and Central England

Coming soon

East Anglia & North London

Scotland

Yorkshire & the North East

If you would like to be notified when certain titles are due for publication please either write to Exploring Woodland Guides, The Woodland Trust, Autumn Park, Dysart Road, Grantham, Lincolnshire NG31 6LL or e-mail woodlandguides@woodland-trust.org.uk

Index

Legal & General is delighted to support the Woodland Trust's conservation programme across the UK.

As a leading UK company, Legal & General recognises the importance of maintaining and improving our environment for future generations. We actively demonstrate our commitment through good management and support of environmental initiatives and organisations, such as the Woodland Trust.

Information on how Legal & General manages its impact on the environment can be found at www.legalandgeneralgroup.com/csr.